B1

PRELIMINARY

FORMULA

FOR EXAM SUCCESS

EXAM TRAINER and eBook

without key

T0386013

CONTENTS

The first page of each exam part begins with a section entitled ABOUT THE TASK. This provides key information about this exam task and its key testing aims.

The first TEST section starts with a mini exam PRACTICE TASK, which is a reduced version of what you will find in the actual B1 Preliminary exam.

The TEACH section provides detailed practice of the strategies and skills required to perform well in the exam part. You are guided through in a systematic, step-by-step way, building on each skill as you progress.

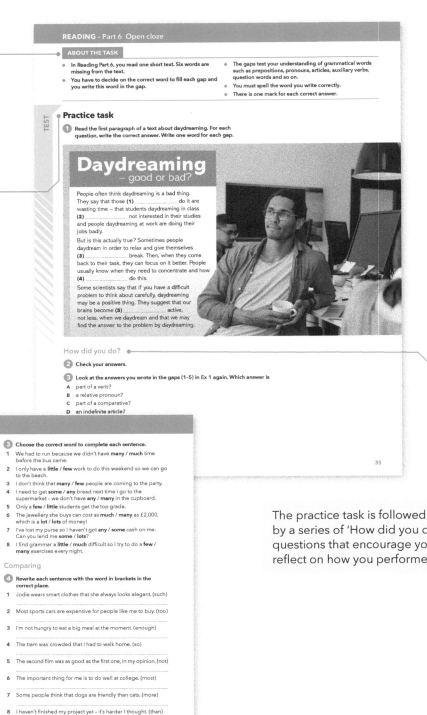

READING - Part 6 Open cloze

ABOUT THE TASK

- In Reading Part 6, you read one short text. Six words are missing from the text.
- You have to decide on the correct word to fill each gap and you write this word in the gap.
- The gaps test your understanding of grammatical words such as prepositions, pronouns, articles, auxiliary verbs, question words and so on.
- You must spell the word you write correctly.
- There is one mark for each correct answer.

Practice task

1. Read the first paragraph of a text about daydreaming. For each question, write the correct answer. Write one word for each gap.

Daydreaming
– good or bad?

People often think daydreaming is a bad thing. They say that those (1) _____ do it are wasting time – that students daydreaming in class (2) _____ not interested in their studies and people daydreaming at work are doing their jobs badly.

But is this actually true? Sometimes people daydream in order to relax and give themselves (3) _____ break. Then, when they come back to their task, they can focus on it better. People usually know when they need to concentrate and how (4) _____ do this.

Some scientists say that if you have a difficult problem to think about carefully, daydreaming may be a positive thing. They suggest that our brains become (5) _____ active, not less, when we daydream and that we may find the answer to the problem by daydreaming.

How did you do?

2. Check your answers.

3. Look at the answers you wrote in the gaps (1-5) in Ex 1 again. Which answer is
   A part of a verb?
   B a relative pronoun?
   C part of a comparative?
   D an indefinite article?

35

READING - Part 6 Open cloze

Strategies and skills

Relative clauses

1. Complete the sentences with the relative pronouns in the box.

   that what where when which who
   whose why

1. I live in a small village _____ everyone knows each other.
2. My sister is a person _____ loves to play tennis.
3. I have no idea _____ to do on Saturday now that my friend isn't coming to stay.
4. We were late so the show had already started _____ we arrived.
5. During the course I studied with Joe, a teacher _____ special interest is ancient history.
6. I wasn't sure _____ the tour was cancelled and no one could tell me the reason.
7. The hotel, _____ was located in the town centre, was fantastic.
8. The show _____ I had originally intended to see was sold out so I couldn't get tickets.

SPEAKING BOOST

Discuss or answer.

1. What time do you usually go to bed? Is it the same in the week as at weekends?
2. In what situations do you find it difficult to get to sleep? What can you do to help?

Articles and quantifiers

2. Complete the paragraph with a, an or the.

My country life

When I woke up it was very early in (1) _____ morning. I got out of bed, went to (2) _____ kitchen and made myself (3) _____ cup of coffee. It was going to be (4) _____ very hot day and I could hear birds singing in (5) _____ trees outside my window. I love living in (6) _____ countryside, even though I have fewer opportunities for entertainment. I used to enjoy (7) _____ evening out with friends, though now I think it's more of (8) _____ advantage to be able to do things like walking and cycling! I think I'm (9) _____ healthiest I've ever been and I don't regret (10) _____ thing about moving here.

36

3. Choose the correct word to complete each sentence.

1. We had to run because we didn't have **many / much** time before the bus came.
2. I only have a **little / few** work to do this weekend so we can go to the beach.
3. I don't think that **many / few** people are coming to the party.
4. I need to get **some / any** bread next time I go to the supermarket – we don't have **any / many** in the cupboard.
5. Only a **few / little** students get the top grade.
6. The jewellery she buys can cost as **much / many** as £2,000, which is a **lot / lots** of money!
7. I've lost my purse so I haven't got **any / some** cash on me. Can you lend me **some / lots**?
8. I find grammar a **little / much** difficult so I try to do a **few / many** exercises every night.

Comparing

4. Rewrite each sentence with the word in brackets in the correct place.

1. Jodie wears smart clothes that she always looks elegant. (such)

2. Most sports cars are expensive for people like me to buy. (too)

3. I'm not hungry to eat a big meal at the moment. (enough)

4. The tram was crowded that I had to walk home. (so)

5. The second film was as good as the first one, in my opinion. (not)

6. The important thing for me is to do well at college. (most)

7. Some people think that dogs are friendly than cats. (more)

8. I haven't finished my project yet - it's harder I thought. (than)

5. Match the sentence beginnings (1-8) with the endings (A-H).

1. I was so busy reading
2. I didn't realise that there would be so
3. The hotter the day,
4. Jose is now one of the world's
5. I love the film - I've seen it
6. I didn't know how difficult
7. I was cold walking home because it was
8. The job would be perfect for someone

A. like my friend Elena.
B. that I missed my station.
C. most popular actors.
D. such a snowy day.
E. the course would be.
F. the more difficult it is to stay cool.
G. more than ten times.
H. many people at the concert.

The practice task is followed by a series of 'How did you do?' questions that encourage you to reflect on how you performed.

In Reading and Listening exam parts, you can find optional Speaking boost tasks. These provide questions to prompt speaking practice in class, or individually at home, to help develop your communicative skills.

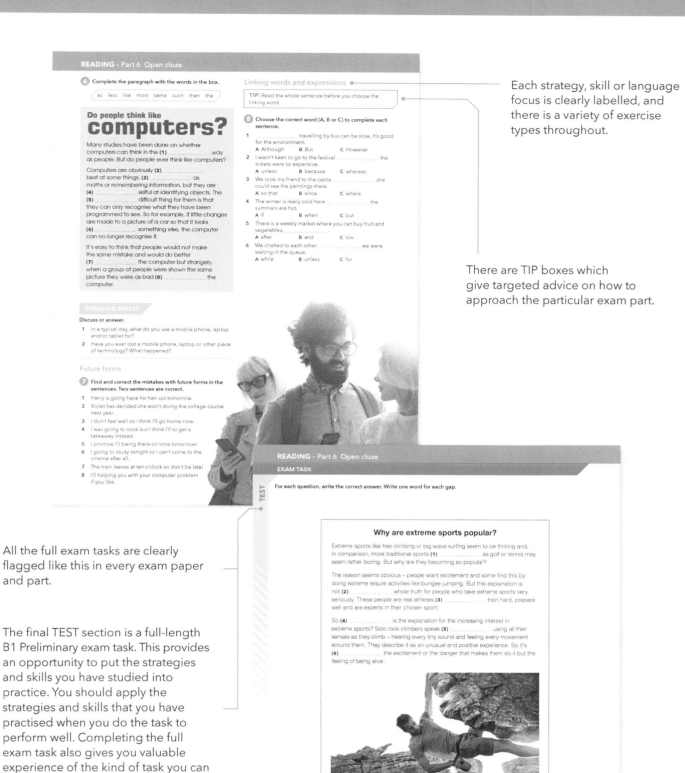

6 Complete the paragraph with the words in the box.

as less like most same such than the

Do people think like
computers?

Many studies have been done on whether computers can think in the (1) _____ way as people. But do people ever think like computers?

Computers are obviously (2) _____ best at some things. (3) _____ as maths or remembering information, but they are (4) _____ skilful at identifying objects. The (5) _____ difficult thing for them is that they can only recognise what they have been programmed to see. So for example, if little changes are made to a picture of a car so that it looks (6) _____ something else, the computer can no longer recognise it.

It's easy to think that people would not make the same mistake and would do better (7) _____ the computer but strangely, when a group of people were shown the same picture they were as bad (8) _____ the computer.

SPEAKING BOOST

Discuss or answer.

1 In a typical day, what do you use a mobile phone, laptop and/or tablet for?

2 Have you ever lost a mobile phone, laptop or other piece of technology? What happened?

Future forms

7 Find and correct the mistakes with future forms in the sentences. Two sentences are correct.

1 Harry is going have his hair cut tomorrow.

2 Violet has decided she won't doing the college course next year.

3 I don't feel well so I think I'll go home now.

4 I was going to cook but I think I'll to get a takeaway instead.

5 I promise I'll being there on time tomorrow!

6 I going to study tonight so I can't come to the cinema after all.

7 The train leaves at ten o'clock so don't be late!

8 I'll helping you with your computer problem if you like.

Linking words and expressions

TIP: Read the whole sentence before you choose the linking word.

8 Choose the correct word (A, B or C) to complete each sentence.

1 _____ travelling by bus can be slow, it's good for the environment.
A Although   B But   C However

2 I wasn't keen to go to the festival _____ the tickets were so expensive.
A unless   B because   C whereas

3 We took my friend to the castle _____ she could see the paintings there.
A so that   B since   C where

4 The winter is really cold here _____ the summers are hot.
A if   B when   C but

5 There is a weekly market where you can buy fruit and vegetables, _____
A after   B and   C too

6 We chatted to each other _____ we were waiting in the queue.
A while   B unless   C for

Each strategy, skill or language focus is clearly labelled, and there is a variety of exercise types throughout.

There are TIP boxes which give targeted advice on how to approach the particular exam part.

For each question, write the correct answer. Write one word for each gap.

Why are extreme sports popular?

Extreme sports like free climbing or big wave surfing seem to be thrilling and, in comparison, more traditional sports (1) _____ as golf or tennis may seem rather boring. But why are they becoming so popular?

The reason seems obvious – people want excitement and some find this by doing extreme leisure activities like bungee jumping. But this explanation is not (2) _____ whole truth for people who take extreme sports very seriously. These people are real athletes (3) _____ train hard, prepare well and are experts in their chosen sport.

So (4) _____ is the explanation for the increasing interest in extreme sports? Solo rock climbers speak (5) _____ using all their senses as they climb – hearing every tiny sound and feeling every movement around them. They describe it as an unusual and positive experience. So it's (6) _____ the excitement or the danger that makes them do it but the feeling of being alive.

All the full exam tasks are clearly flagged like this in every exam paper and part.

The final TEST section is a full-length B1 Preliminary exam task. This provides an opportunity to put the strategies and skills you have studied into practice. You should apply the strategies and skills that you have practised when you do the task to perform well. Completing the full exam task also gives you valuable experience of the kind of task you can expect to find in the Cambridge B1 Preliminary exam.

An Answer Key for all tasks is provided, either in the back of your book or via the Pearson English Portal.

All audioscripts are printed in the back of the book.

What is *Formula*?

Formula is a brand-new exam preparation course that provides teachers and learners with unrivalled flexibility in exam training. The course offers complete and extensive preparation for the Cambridge B1 Preliminary, B2 First and C1 Advanced exams. The core materials provide thorough, step-by-step targeted exam training, helping learners to develop a deeper understanding of the strategies and skills needed to succeed. Comprehensive practice of these skills and strategies for each exam task type is systematically provided through engaging, contemporary topics.

The course comprises two core components: the **Coursebook** and the **Exam Trainer**. These can be used as stand-alone components, or together, depending on the learning environment.

Both course components are suitable for the standard and 'For Schools' versions of the Cambridge English exams.

What is the *Formula* B1 Preliminary Exam Trainer?

The *Formula* **B1 Preliminary Exam Trainer** is specially designed to maximise your chances of success in the Cambridge B1 Preliminary or B1 Preliminary for Schools examinations.

It can work either as a standalone component or in combination with the *Formula* **B1 Preliminary Coursebook**. Its structure follows the Cambridge B1 Preliminary exam, working systematically through each Paper and Part, from Reading Part 1 to Speaking Part 4. Each Paper is introduced with a detailed overview of the exam task format, followed by a 'Test, Teach, Test' approach, to improve understanding and performance.

The Test, Teach, Test approach

TEST: A mini 'practice task' that reflects the Cambridge B1 Preliminary exam task for that Part, with a 'How did you do?' reflection activity. This helps learners familiarise themselves with the task type and quickly highlights any obvious focus for improving performance.

TEACH: An extensive series of explanations, tips and targeted tasks to practise the strategies and skills for improving performance in the exam. The skills are organised in priority order, so students with little time know which sections to focus on first to gain maximum effect.

TEST: A full-length, authentic-style exam task to put the exam training to the test, with a full, 'smart' answer key.

At the back of the Exam Trainer there is also a full, authentic-style Cambridge B1 Preliminary exam, with accompanying audio. We advise that this exam is taken under exam conditions when the training phase is complete.

All audio for the Exam Trainer is available via the App on the Pearson English Portal. The audio is available for download so you can save it to your device to listen offline.

How can I use the *Formula* B1 Preliminary Exam Trainer?

The *Formula* **B1 Preliminary Exam Trainer** is a flexible component and can be used effectively in a number of different learning environments. Here are some typical situations:

You are studying for the Cambridge B1 Preliminary exam with other students in a classroom scenario, probably over an academic year.

You are using the *Formula* **B1 Preliminary Coursebook** in class. Sometimes you will also do the related exercises or even a whole exam part from the *Formula* **B1 Preliminary Exam Trainer** in class, though your teacher will ask you to do exercises from it at home as well. You will use the entire **Exam Trainer** or you will use it selectively, depending on your needs and the time available.

You have already completed a Cambridge B1 Preliminary exam course or general B1-level English course. You are enrolled on an intensive exam preparation course with other students to do targeted exam practice.

You may have already worked though the *Formula* **B1 Preliminary Coursebook** or perhaps another Cambridge B1 Preliminary coursebook. You will use the *Formula* **B1 Preliminary Exam Trainer** in class to give you a concentrated and highly focused short exam course. This will provide systematic, teacher-led exam training paper by paper, with Speaking boosts for communicative activities in class. You may focus on the exam sections in class, and the skills and strategies at home, or the reverse. There is also a full, authentic-style Practice Exam included in the title, which you can sit under exam conditions prior to taking the exam.

You only have a short time available to prepare for the Cambridge B1 Preliminary exam and are not enrolled in an exam preparation course.

You have been attending general English classes and your level of English is already nearing Cambridge B1 Preliminary exam standard. You now need targeted exam skills practice. You will use the *Formula* **B1 Preliminary Exam Trainer** independently to work through each of the exam papers in order, so that you are familiar with the exam tasks and equipped with key strategies for improving your performance. The Speaking boost sections provide valuable speaking practice and the full, authentic-style Practice Exam can be sat under exam conditions prior to taking the exam.

You only have a short time available and are preparing for the Cambridge B1 Preliminary exam on your own.

Maybe you are not attending English classes at present but wish to take the Cambridge B1 Preliminary exam and prepare for it independently. You will use the *Formula* **B1 Preliminary Exam Trainer** independently to work through each of the exam papers in order, so that you are familiar with the exam tasks and equipped with key strategies for improving your performance. The Speaking boost sections provide valuable speaking practice and the full, authentic-style Practice Exam can be sat under exam conditions prior to taking the exam.

- In Reading Part 1, you read five short texts on different topics. These texts are taken from real-world situations, including signs, notices, messages, emails and so on.
- You identify the meaning of the text.

- Each question has three multiple-choice options (A, B and C) for you to choose from.
- You choose the option that is most similar in meaning to the text.

Practice task

1 For each question, choose the correct answer.

1

> No noise between 11 p.m. and 7 a.m. Please come and go quietly during this time so you don't annoy other people.

A Be quiet if you are moving about late at night.
B You can't come in after 11 p.m.
C Don't make a noise after 7 in the morning.

2

> Bicycle for sale. One owner, hardly used, only £200. Also two helmets, prices to be discussed.

A The bicycle and helmets cost £200.
B The bicycle can be bought without the helmets.
C The bicycle has been used a lot so is cheap.

3

> Al, I've ordered a new computer game from the shop in town. I've already paid for it, so could you pick it up when you're there tomorrow?
>
> Jan

A Jan wants Al to go to town the next day to order a computer game.
B Jan wants to give some money to Al to buy a computer game.
C Jan wants Al to collect a computer game the next day.

4

> A scarf was left in the lecture hall and is now at reception. If you've lost one, please come to collect it.

A Go to reception if you've found a scarf anywhere.
B There's a scarf missing from the lecture hall.
C Anyone looking for a scarf should go to reception.

How did you do?

2 Check your answers.

3 Look at Ex 1 question 1. Answer the questions below.

1 What is it?
   A an advertisement   B a notice   C an email
2 Where might you see it?
   A a library   B a block of flats   C a swimming pool
3 Look at option A.
   A Does it mention 11 p.m.?
   B Does it mention being able to come in or go out at night?
4 Look at option B.
   A Does it mention people who live there?
   B Does it mention residents making a noise themselves?
5 Look at option C.
   A Does it ask you to be quiet?
   B Does it mention night time?

4 Look at Ex 1 question 2. Answer the questions below.

1 What is it?
   A a text   B an advertisement   C an email
2 Where might you see it?
   A a newspaper   B a computer   C a mobile phone
3 Look at option A.
   A Does it mention how much the bicycle cost originally?
   B Does it mention how to buy the bicycle?
4 Look at option B.
   A Does it mention the cost of the bicycle itself?
   B Does it mention that you can buy the bicycle and helmets separately?
5 Look at option C.
   A Does it say that the bicycle was ridden a lot?
   B Does it say the bicycle is cheap?

5 Look at Ex 1 question 3. Answer the questions below.

1 A Who wrote the text message?
   B Who received the text message?
2 A Who ordered the computer game?
   B Who is going into town?

6 Look at Ex 1 question 4. Are the statements below true or false?

1 The scarf has been lost.
2 The scarf is now in the lecture hall.
3 The scarf is now at reception.
4 We know who the scarf belongs to.
5 The owner of the scarf needs to go to reception.

TEACH

Strategies and skills
Time expressions

TIP: Signs and short messages often mention specific times or periods of time. It's important to understand time expressions in order to understand the meaning correctly.

1 Which option (A or B) has the same meaning as the original sentence?

1 The lesson will continue until 3 p.m.
   A The lesson will finish at 3 p.m.
   B The lesson will finish before 3 p.m.

2 Don't enter the room until you see a green light.
   A You can enter the room after you see a green light.
   B You can enter the room before there is a green light.

3 You should arrive by 5 p.m. at the latest.
   A You can arrive after 5 p.m.
   B You can arrive any time up to 5 p.m.

4 The shop is open between 9 a.m. and 5 p.m. every day.
   A The shop closes at 5 p.m.
   B The shop opens before 9 a.m.

5 The bus is due to arrive in ten minutes.
   A The bus won't arrive after ten minutes.
   B The bus will not arrive until ten minutes have passed.

6 You must not use phones during the performance.
   A You can use phones when the performance is happening.
   B You can use phones before and after the performance.

2 Complete the sentences with the time expressions in the box.

> at the latest   before   between   by   due   during
> earliest   in advance   until   while

1 The surgery is open _____ 8 a.m. and 5 p.m.

2 Tickets will go on sale on 1st March at the _____ .

3 Your final payment for the holiday is _____ to be paid on 20th May.

4 Wait _____ your name is called before approaching the reception area.

5 Taking photographs _____ the performance is strictly forbidden.

6 Switch off all mobile phones _____ the concert is in progress.

7 Please return all application forms by Friday _____ to enter the competition.

8 You can buy tickets _____ online.

9 The cinema will open 30 minutes _____ the film starts.

10 The show will be finished _____ 10 p.m.

SPEAKING BOOST

Discuss or answer.

1 Think about a typical weekday or weekend for you. What things do you do at certain times of the day?

2 Imagine your ideal holiday. Say what you do in the mornings, afternoons and evenings.

Understanding the main message

TIP: Think about what the purpose and main message of each text is and where you might see it. This helps you to use the context when you think about the meaning.

3 For each statement, choose the correct ending.

1 A sign
   A gives personal information to a friend.
   B gives information to the public in a public place.

2 An advertisement
   A tells people about a product they can buy.
   B tells people what they can and can't do.

3 An instruction
   A tells people what to do or how to do it.
   B describes something that is happening.

4 A notice
   A explains a product and says how much it costs.
   B is often temporary and gives specific information about a situation.

5 A personal message
   A is usually written in informal language from one person to another.
   B is the same as a formal letter to a company.

4 Choose the correct context for each sentence.

1 Please keep off the grass. **sign / advertisement**

2 Complete the form using black ink. **instruction / email**

3 Please close the door quietly after leaving the building. **notice / text message**

4 Take one tablet a day with food. **text message / instruction from doctor**

5 I'll be late tonight so go ahead and have dinner without me. **notice / personal message**

6 Ball games are not allowed in the park. **advertisement / sign**

7 All bread is on special offer this week – only £1 from Jones the Baker! **instruction / advertisement**

8 Everyone must report to the reception desk on the ground floor on arrival. **email / sign**

KEEP OFF THE GRASS

5 **Match the personal messages with the functions in the box.**

> complaining about something
> describing something   explaining something
> giving an instruction   giving an invitation
> making an offer   making a request
> recommending something
> reminding someone of something
> suggesting something

1 Hi! Could you put the milk in the fridge when you get home, please? I forgot to do it.

2 You must arrive before 6 p.m., as the doors close at 6.15 p.m.

3 I'm sorry but I'll be late tonight because the train was cancelled.

4 I can collect the book from the library if you like – I'm going past there this afternoon.

5 Don't forget to buy the bread on your way home.

6 Why don't you come round on Sunday? We can have lunch together.

7 The shirt I bought Peter for his birthday was blue with small yellow stripes.

8 I went shopping yesterday but the traffic was terrible!

9 We haven't decided what to do tomorrow – why don't we play tennis?

10 That was such a great film – I think you should definitely see it. You'll love it!

6 **What is the function of each sign? Choose A or B.**

1 Please enter using the right-hand door.
   A explaining how to use the right-hand door
   B asking you to use the right-hand door

2 Do not ride bikes on the pavement.
   A telling you where you are not allowed to ride bikes
   B suggesting where you can ride bikes

3 The 35 bus has been cancelled.
   A complaining about the bus service
   B giving information about the bus service

4 Please pay for your food when you order it.
   A describing how you pay for your food
   B giving an instruction about paying for your food

5 Don't go to the departure gate until your flight is announced.
   A asking you to go to the departure gate now
   B reminding you not to go to the departure gate too early

6 Turn off all mobile phones during the performance.
   A instructing you to turn off your phone
   B suggesting when you can use your phone

The language of signs

> **TIP:** When you read signs, they may have some words missing but you can still work out their meaning.

Signs are often expressed in the shortest way possible, so they leave out words such as articles or verbs.

7 **Replace the words left out from the signs below using the words and phrases in the box. There may be more than one possible answer.**

> a   are   has been   is   is to be used   the   there are   will

1 Please don't block entrance.
_____

2 Cars parked here without permit will be removed.
_____

3 This recycling bin for paper only.
_____

4 The 4.30 train delayed by 30 minutes by a signal failure.
_____

5 Orders received by next Friday get a 10 percent discount.
_____

6 The library now closed until Wednesday morning.
_____

7 Temporary speed limits in place for 3 kilometres.
_____

8 All cakes now on sale at reduced prices.
_____

Giving permission and giving orders

8 **Complete the sentences with the words in the box.**

> allowed   available   can   have
> must   not   provided   unless

1 You _____ to show an ID card if you want to get a discount.

2 Tickets are _____ online or at the box office.

3 You _____ only use cameras in selected parts of the museum.

4 Cycling is only _____ on the marked paths.

5 Please put all litter in the bins _____ near the exit.

6 Cameras _____ not be used in the theatre.

7 Ball games are _____ allowed anywhere in the park.

8 You can't use the sports centre _____ you are a member.

For each question, choose the correct answer.

1

Free parking from 6 p.m. to 8 a.m., and on Sundays. At all other times, buy a ticket at the machine or text 00885.

A You can only park when you buy a ticket.
B It's not necessary to buy a ticket every day.
C There is only one way to buy a ticket.

2

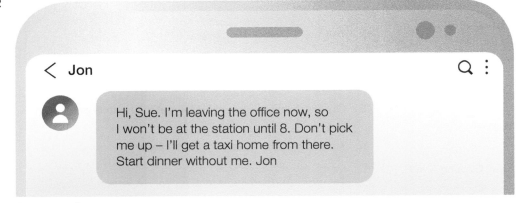

> < Jon   🔍 ⋮
>
> Hi, Sue. I'm leaving the office now, so I won't be at the station until 8. Don't pick me up – I'll get a taxi home from there. Start dinner without me. Jon

Jon wants Sue to
A begin eating before he gets home.
B meet him at the office after 8.
C come to collect him from the station.

3

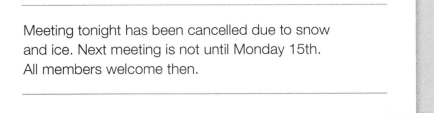

Meeting tonight has been cancelled due to snow and ice. Next meeting is not until Monday 15th. All members welcome then.

A The next meeting will take place sometime before Monday 15th.
B All members have to attend the next meeting unless it snows.
C The weather is too bad for tonight's meeting to take place.

4

> Pay for James Wilson's
> latest book in-store or online to
> get it as soon as it's published.
> Other books half price.

A You can buy all new books at a discount.
B You can order the new book now.
C You can only buy the new book online.

5

👤 **From:** Jack
Subject: Concert tickets

Hi Andy,

I've checked the ticket prices on the concert website and they're expensive.
I'd rather see if there's a special offer on another site. I don't want to pay too much.

Jack

A Jack is hoping that the tickets will be cheaper elsewhere.
B Jack is suggesting that he will have to pay a lot for the tickets.
C Jack is asking Andy to buy tickets for him for the concert.

TEST

- In Reading Part 2, there are eight short texts. These texts are all on the same topic and have similar information and ideas.
- Some examples of the topics for the short texts might be holidays, courses, reviews of films and so on.
- You are given information about five different people who are all interested in the topics of the eight short texts.
- You match the information given in the texts with the appropriate person. There are three texts that don't match any of the people.
- There is one mark for each correct answer.

Practice task

1 For each question, choose the correct answer.

The people below want to visit a place near the sea.

There are descriptions of five places near the sea.

Decide which place would be most suitable for the people below.

1 Crista is keen on photography and would like to take photographs of wildlife. She loves walking by the sea, and hopes to find cheap accommodation with sea views.

2 Francesco is planning to swim in the sea and stay in a hotel on cliffs overlooking the ocean. He's also interested in finding out about how the town developed in the past.

A Freshwater

If you're looking for water sports, this is the perfect place, and it's perfectly safe for all ages. There are other sports available, too, including tennis and badminton. There's live entertainment in the local theatre every night and an excellent museum for anyone interested in history. Our good-quality hotels provide luxury and the opportunity to relax.

B Marineville

The water here is perfect for swimmers, so why not improve your diving skills with our experienced instructors? Our hotels have high standards, but are not expensive, and they're situated on the cliffs with fantastic sea views. There's a fireworks display on the beach once a month, too. For historians, information on the area can be found in the museum.

C Stevton

This is the place to come if you're a keen photographer of landscapes as the views of the mountains behind the town are amazing. Why not stay in a hostel up there for a change? You can walk or cycle and enjoy the fresh air. For a special meal, try one of the mountain restaurants with amazing beef dishes.

D Oldquay

Visitors love the views of birds from the cliffs, and if you're lucky, you can see dolphins, too. Make sure you have your camera so you can take that special picture of them. There are marked paths for walking or cycling. Anyone wanting to save money can stay on the campsite overlooking the sea and enjoy a barbecue. Why not have a swim, too?

How did you do?

2 Check your answers.

3 Look at the highlighted parts in the text about Oldquay in Ex 1. Match these with one of the two people. Check the answer.

4 Look at the description of Francesco in Ex 1. Tick the three things he wants.
- swimming
- a hotel with a sea view
- fish restaurants
- local history
- evening concerts

5 Underline the relevant parts of the text about Marineville that match the things Francesco wants.

Strategies and skills

Understanding what someone wants, likes or needs

> **TIP:** Underline the important information about each person. This helps you remember what you're looking for in the texts.

It's important to identify what each person likes, prefers, needs or doesn't want so you can match them with the right text.

1 Read the information about five people who are going to spend a weekend in the countryside. Underline the words that tell you what each person likes, dislikes, prefers or needs.

1 Jo loves spending time by lakes and mountains and is fascinated by plants and flowers. She can't afford to stay in a hotel so she is looking for a cheap hostel.

2 Ali is keen on seeing local wildlife, especially wildlife that lives in forests. He only likes exploring on his own, and taking photographs.

3 Clara loves being in the countryside but is afraid of high places. She prefers to stay in good-quality large hotels but hates being in crowds.

4 Leo would like to go camping because he loves being in the fresh air. He dislikes hotels and loves barbecues. He doesn't want to use a car and tries to cycle everywhere.

5 Ella is interested in joining a trip to a large national park. She wants to learn about wildlife so she needs a guide. She's happy to travel by bus but would like to spend time on foot in the forest.

2 Are the following statements true or false? Correct those that are false.

1 Jo is interested in animals.

2 Ali would enjoy being part of a group.

3 Clara doesn't mind paying extra for better accommodation.

4 Leo enjoys cooking outside.

5 Ella only wants to get around by bus.

3 Look at all the descriptions again. Which person

1 doesn't like being in the mountains?

2 hopes to do some walking?

3 likes to spend as much time as possible outside?

4 needs to take a camera?

5 hasn't got much money?

6 wants to avoid driving?

7 is keen to go with an expert?

8 doesn't want to be in a tour group?

9 is unhappy in a large group?

10 likes to be near water?

SPEAKING BOOST

Discuss or answer.

1 Describe your favourite place and why it is special to you.

2 What's the best way to travel around a city when you visit? Give reasons.

Matching words and ideas

> **TIP:** You may not see the same words in the profiles of the people and in the descriptions. Think about the exact meaning of each one.

The profiles of the people are often written in quite a general way. The information in the descriptions is more specific and includes details that help you match the description with the right person.

4 Match the general profile information (1–10) with the details (A–J).

1 Andi wants to do different sports.

2 Helen likes to get away from her busy city life.

3 Gina enjoys films.

4 Ali wants to buy a new book.

5 Sue wants to get fit.

6 Angel enjoys cycling.

7 Max would like to eat different types of food.

8 Maria wants to learn more about art.

9 Izner is disappointed with his photographs.

10 Isabel wants to stay in nice accommodation.

A You'll have the choice of five large screens as well as a café.

B Our cosy rooms are clean and comfortable.

C Here you can choose from the latest best-sellers.

D There are tennis courts and hockey pitches in the town.

E There's a gym with various classes you can join for a fee.

F Why not take a relaxing walk in the countryside?

G We will study the work of people like Picasso.

H The local restaurants serve dishes from all over the world.

I There are bikes for hire near the museum.

J After our course you'll take better pictures.

5 Read the profiles of two people who both want to have a winter holiday. What general information do you know about each person? Underline it.

1 Peter loves speed! His favourite sport is skiing but he's also good at skating. He has just started rock climbing and wants to learn more about it with experts. He can only afford to stay in a cheap hotel.

2 Jane isn't keen on exercise although she enjoys swimming. She likes the mountains because there, she can forget any stress in her life. She wants places to go in the evenings and likes buying things for friends.

6 Here are some details about things that are important for people who want a winter holiday. Match the details with Peter or Jane. There are two ideas you don't need to use.

1 There's a bus between different mountain resorts every day.

2 There are lessons with experienced climbing instructors.

3 Relax and enjoy the clean air of the mountains!

4 There are many places for meeting friends at the end of the day.

5 An indoor skating rink is open every day.

6 You can borrow equipment from the hotel reception.

7 Take part in races down the mountain slopes!

8 Enjoy the big indoor pool, which is open to everyone.

9 There are plenty of places to buy clothes and gifts.

10 The hotels are not expensive.

7 Complete the full descriptions of the best holidays for Jane and Peter using the words in the box. Which one is for Jane and which one is for Peter?

> cheaper   experienced   pool   races
> restaurants   school   shopping centre
> skating   souvenirs   theatre

Hotels here are **(1)** _____ than in other resorts. Skiers can take part in **(2)** _____ every Friday. There's no entry fee and everyone's welcome - as long as you're good! Alternatively, you can go **(3)** _____ . We've just opened a climbing **(4)** _____ so if you've never tried it before, why not come along? Our instructors are all very **(5)** _____ .

You don't have to ski to enjoy this beautiful mountain town in the winter. There are cafés and **(6)** _____ where you can relax with friends at the end of the day and there's even a **(7)** _____ with regular shows. If you're keen on swimming, there's a large indoor **(8)** _____ and a **(9)** _____ where you can find lovely gifts and **(10)** _____ .

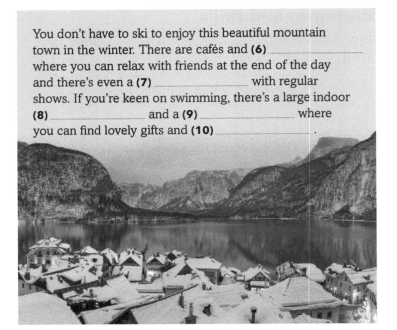

Identifying information that is not relevant

You should always choose the correct description for each person by deciding what that person wants or likes. However, if you are not sure, it can also be useful to identify information that is not relevant.

8 The people below all want to join a dance class. Read their profiles and choose the correct answer in each option.

1 Ayesha wants to join a class that includes ballet and hip hop, although she's not interested in jazz. She would like to see some dance performances and take some dance exams.

2 Hari can only attend classes in the evenings and is interested in modern dance and jazz. He wants to learn more about famous dancers.

3 Maria wants to learn about music as well as dance. She is hoping that the classes will help her to keep fit and she's hoping to take part in some performances on stage.

1 What does Ayesha want to do?
   A ballet   B some modern dance   C both
   A watch dance shows B take part in them   C both
   A take exams   B not take exams   C have fun

2 What does Hari want to do?
   A have classes in the   B have classes in the   C both
     evenings   mornings
   A learn ballet   B learn modern dance   C learn both
   A find out about   B meet other dancers   C both
     famous dancers

3 What does Maria want to do?
   A learn about music   B learn about dance   C both
   A keep fit   B get stronger   C both
   A perform in a show   B watch a show   C both

9 Answer the questions below about Text A in Ex 10.

1 Look the information about Ayesha. Does Text A mention any of the things she wants? If so, underline them.

2 Look at the information about Hari. Does Text A mention any of the things he wants? If so, underline them.

3 Look at the information about Maria. Does Text A mention any of the things she wants? If so, underline them.

4 Does Text A match any person completely?

> **TIP:** If Text A does not give you all the information you need about one person or there is information in Text A that you have not underlined, then that information is not relevant so you can move on. The text you choose must match <u>all</u> the information in the profile of the person.

10 Text A does not match any of the three people. Now read texts B–E and decide which dance class would be most suitable for each person.

A All About Dance

Have you ever wanted to learn modern dance? If so, these are the classes for you! Spend your Wednesday mornings in our school in the town centre and you'll feel healthier and happier for it. Although we don't enter students for any tests or put on any shows, the standard is very high and everyone has a good time.

B Top Dance Studio

We are proud that some well-known dancers started their careers in our studio and they have become role models for our younger students. Some return and give talks about themselves and their careers and even teach some classes. We are only able to offer ballet classes during the day but classes in all other types of dance begin at 6 p.m.

C Point College

Although our teachers have some experience in all dance forms, our most popular classes are ballet. These classes take place during the day and at weekends and cost £25 for two hours. We often organise trips to watch ballet, usually on Saturday evenings, and all students are welcome because we feel this helps them improve their own dancing technique.

D Ann's Dance Academy

Our classes cover a range of dance types, including modern and more traditional. We want our students to reach the highest standards they can and get some qualifications that will give them confidence and also encourage them to improve. Every month we take students to the theatre to watch a show and we talk about the moves with them in our classes.

E Swan Dance School

Of course dance classes are an excellent way to exercise and keep fit but we believe they are more than that. We teach students how to dance, help them understand what they are dancing to and how that makes them feel. Dance should be enjoyed by people doing it and also by those watching it, so we perform shows regularly. Everyone has the chance to take part.

11 Tick the information from texts A–E that is not relevant to any of the three people.

- cost of classes
- music
- morning classes
- location of school
- exams

For each question, choose the correct answer.

The young people below all want to join a club for people who enjoy films.

On the opposite page there are descriptions of eight film clubs.

Decide which club would be most suitable for the people below.

1

Jack wants a club where members get together regularly to discuss films face-to-face. He enjoys films with songs in them and likes to go on organised trips to watch a film.

2

Beth prefers serious films and doesn't like comedies or musicals. She wants to find out more about the background to films she watches and to get recommendations for other films.

3

Andy prefers independent films to famous blockbusters and wants to attend organised talks by directors and actors online. He enjoys posting his own reviews of films he's seen.

4

Carrie loves films about animals. She's very interested in the technical side of making films and wants to find out more about this. She wants to take part in an online discussion forum.

5

Josh wants to start his own blog about films he's seen. He loves science fiction and wants ideas from other fans for books to read with similar stories to the films.

Film clubs

A Film Fans

Our club meetings on Thursday evenings are social occasions as well as opportunities for serious discussion. The range of films we like is wide, from science fiction to musicals, and we publish the list of those we will watch every six months. Members are free to recommend films we can include in the following months.

B Cinema Group

We meet every Tuesday evening in the café of the local cinema. Members discuss films they've seen in the past online or in the cinema and talk about what they liked or didn't like about them. Once a month there's a trip to see a special film chosen by the group, which is often a musical and is always a fun event.

C Film Club

We arrange online question and answer sessions with directors and actors who introduce us to unusual and fascinating films, such as strange films about life in the future. They really make you think! There's a link on our website for members to write their opinions of films they've seen. On the whole, we prefer films from small companies to big blockbusters.

D Film World

Many of our members are fascinated by nature and will watch anything with wildlife in it. We explore the difficulties of making films like this and how these problems are solved by film-makers. There's a part of our site where users can chat about films they've seen and many members write their opinions on the general website so that we can all share them.

E Screen Fans

We welcome film fans who want to share their ideas and experiences. We meet weekly in the local cinema and after watching a film we write down our thoughts. These appear in the club's monthly newsletter for other members to discuss. We also have a monthly competition to win free cinema tickets.

F Crazy About Films

We're into any film showing life in the future or on other planets. We meet every month to talk about them and because they're often based on novels we talk about those, too, and suggest ones like them to read. It's great when members write up their own opinions of films and some have their own blogs, which we all enjoy reading.

G Watch It

Many members belong to the local wildlife association and there's a particular interest in watching films about the natural world. This includes scientific documentaries about the stars and life on other planets. We run competitions every month and occasional trips to local wildlife parks. Some people even show their own films of animal life or the stars!

H Love Films

We want to have fun but that doesn't mean watching funny films! We prefer dramas and we often meet and read the scripts together. Members research facts behind these, which helps us understand them, and we invite young directors to post online about their work. The site has an excellent recommendations section where members can add their ideas.

TEST

ABOUT THE TASK

- In Reading Part 3, you read one long text. This could be about a person, an event, an experience, etc.
- There are five multiple-choice questions about the text. You choose the correct answer to each question from four options (A, B, C and D).

- Four questions ask about details, feelings, attitudes or opinions expressed by the writer or by someone mentioned in the text.
- The fifth question asks a question about the text as a whole.
- There is one mark for each correct answer.

Practice task

1 Read three paragraphs from an article about children and their use of technology such as tablets and mobile phones. For each question, choose the correct answer.

1 What does the writer do in the first paragraph?
  A describe how tablets are generally used
  B complain about the current cost of tablets
  C remind readers of who uses tablets most
  D question the use of tablets by young children

2 How does the writer feel about controlling children's use of tablets?
  A He is glad that it is not done all the time.
  B He is pleased when people recommend it.
  C He regrets the lack of evidence for it.
  D He is worried about the way it is often done.

3 In the third paragraph, the writer thinks that for young children, technology can be
  A a useful way to learn.
  B as good as a teacher.
  C an easy way to contact friends.
  D an enjoyable form of entertainment.

4 What would the writer say about the way tablets are used by young children?
  A I wish people discussed the problem more so that it could be solved.
  B I disagree with the idea that they should be used in schools.
  C I realise there are advantages and disadvantages to children using technology in general.
  D I don't like the way people often criticise young children who use them.

How did you do?

2 Check your answers.

3 Look at the options in question 1 and paragraph 1 in Ex 1. Answer the questions below.

  1 The writer mentions tablets but does he describe how they are used?

  2 The writer mentions that tablets used to be expensive but is he complaining about this?

  3 The writer says that tablets have advantages but does he remind readers about who uses them most?

  4 The writer says that young children use tablets but does he say this is a good thing or does he question it?

4 Look at the highlighted parts of paragraph 2 and the options in question 2 in Ex 1 that each one refers to. Why is B right? Why are the other options wrong?

5 Look at the options in question 3 and paragraph 3 in Ex 1. Highlight the part of the text that refers to option A. Why is A the right answer?

6 Look at the whole text again. Ex 1 question 4 is asking about the writer's opinion in the whole text, not one particular paragraph. Think about his opinion throughout the article. Is he generally positive about tablets or negative?

TECHNOLOGY AND YOUNG CHILDREN

Inventions tend to become cheaper as they become more widely used, and touch devices like tablets are much less expensive than they used to be. They're everywhere and offer enormous advantages in daily life for work and leisure. But now it seems that the age children are using them has become much younger. I've seen tiny toddlers swiping through apps as if it's the most natural thing in the world, and this may not be a good thing.

Some parents stop children under two from using technology and others limit how much they are allowed to use it. This may be because they know a child's brain is growing quickly under the age of three and are afraid that technology could damage it. Although there's no definite proof that technology has any negative effects like this, a young child might find using technology more enjoyable than playing with other children and this could stop them making relationships and learning social skills. So even if children don't like it, it's not a bad thing when people suggest reducing screen time, and technical skills can be learnt when the child is older.

Some people say that far from limiting social development, technology gets children working, talking and problem-solving together. Clearly, if teachers use technology correctly, especially in the classroom, it can only improve a child's ability to learn. Using tablets must be fun for young children and even if they're only playing games with friends, becoming familiar with technology will prepare them to do well later on. Nevertheless, people who think that tablets are unsuitable for young children are still not convinced.

Strategies and skills

Identifying attitude and opinion

> **TIP:** In the text, you won't read words such as 'worried' or 'happy' if they are in the options. You will read other words or phrases that tell you how the writer feels.

Questions ask about the attitude, feelings or opinion of the writer or of a person in the text. You need to think about the words people use to express their feelings and their opinions about something.

1 Look at the short blog below. Are statements 1–6 true or false? Underline the words that give you the answer.

1 Jose was disappointed by his trip to Australia.

2 Jose felt worried about travelling around.

3 Jose was annoyed by some other travellers.

4 Jose didn't like the traffic in the city.

5 Jose liked the beaches he visited.

6 Jose was surprised by the variety of wildlife he saw.

MY AUSTRALIAN TRIP

I'd spent such a long time looking forward to my visit to Australia that when I finally got there it wasn't quite as good as I expected.

Obviously, Australia's a very big country and it took a long time to get from one place to another. Although that was boring sometimes it wasn't really a problem and it didn't make me feel anxious at all. One long journey I remember was on a bus and some of the passengers were playing really loud music the whole time. I hate it when people do that, especially when I'm trying to get some sleep! The traffic in the cities was pretty bad, too, which was a shame – it sometimes took ages to get out of the centre.

There were many great things about the trip, though. There were beautiful sandy beaches where I spent a lot of time, and the surfing there was amazing. I got quite good at it! I had several trips out into the countryside and I couldn't believe how many kangaroos there were in the wild – they looked really cute! I took loads of photographs of them.

2 Read the sentences. Which word (A, B or C) describes how the writer felt?

1 I love travelling and I couldn't wait to get to the airport.
   A disappointed   **B** excited   **C** nervous

2 I went to the cinema with my friend but I couldn't understand what was going on at all – the story was so complicated.
   A annoyed   **B** worried   **C** confused

3 I expected the course to be difficult and on the first day I wasn't sure I could do it.
   A nervous   **B** surprised   **C** excited

4 The lecture seemed to go on for ages – I just wanted it to end.
   A sad   **B** bored   **C** keen

5 I was so pleased to get home after the long journey – I was so tired.
   A bored   **B** annoyed   **C** relieved

6 The art gallery had so many beautiful pictures – I've never seen such a wonderful collection.
   A confused   **B** impressed   **C** frightened

3 Read the paragraphs and answer the questions about the writer's opinion.

> I was convinced about doing the course because I love music and the chance to learn a new musical instrument was too good to miss. It was just a shame that the lessons took place on Saturday mornings so I couldn't go to hockey training then. I don't regret it, though.

1 What is the writer's opinion about the decision he made to do the course?
   A It was a good one.
   B It was difficult to make.

> It's fun to eat in a new restaurant and when one opened in town I was keen to try it. The menu looked good and I decided to go with a group of friends. We booked a table and hoped to have a great evening. It didn't work out that way, though. The service was poor and the food was even worse. I shall do some research before trying anywhere new again!

2 What does the writer think about going to a new restaurant?
   A It's always a good idea.
   B It can be a mistake.

> I had an accident at work and hurt my right wrist very badly. I'm right-handed, so suddenly doing even simple things became difficult. Getting dressed, using a pen, doing up buttons – these took ages, but the hardest thing was using a pair of scissors! I had a lot of help from my family and friends but they didn't realise how many problems I had.

3 What does the writer think about having the injury?
   A It was impossible for other people to understand the difficulties.
   B It was necessary to ask for help in that situation.

SPEAKING BOOST

Discuss or answer.

1 What rules about the use of technology did you have when you were young?

2 What are your favourite apps? What do they do and how often do you use them?

Understanding global meaning

> **TIP:** In the exam, the last question refers to the whole text, not to one particular paragraph. You need to look for information in different parts of the text to find the answer and it will not be stated clearly.

Sometimes a writer doesn't state something clearly and you have to understand what they mean in general.

4 Look at the short paragraphs. They don't give an exact opinion. What would the writer say about each one? Choose A or B.

1 It rained all day so I couldn't do what I had planned. I stayed in the house and watched television. The day seemed to go on forever. I don't want to waste time like that again, even though some people might think it was nice not to feel any pressure.

   A I felt so bored the whole day.
   B It was a relaxing day when I did nothing.

2 The match started well and all the players were trying really hard. At that point it was exciting to watch and I even thought we had a chance of winning. Then the other team scored a goal and from that moment everything went wrong. We were never going to win!

   A I was disappointed about the way my team played.
   B I enjoyed parts of the game.

3 The traffic was so bad on Saturday that it was difficult to find a parking space in the town. When I got to the shopping centre all the shops were really crowded and it was impossible to walk around without bumping into people. I didn't manage to buy anything I wanted and then it took ages to drive home!

   A I wish I hadn't gone shopping.
   B I like shopping in town on a Saturday.

4 The holiday started badly, with the journey to the airport taking twice as long as normal because of the heavy traffic. Everyone was feeling annoyed by the time we actually got onto the plane. Then the flight was more uncomfortable than any other one I can remember and when we arrived at the resort it was raining – they said it had never rained in July before!

   A Going on holiday is usually an enjoyable experience.
   B Long-distance travelling is never much fun.

Reading for detailed comprehension

When you do the task, you should read each part of the text carefully. You then match the exact meaning of what you read with the meaning of one of the options.

5 Read the paragraphs carefully. Only one option (A–C) is true. Choose the correct option. Why are the others not true?

1 Roberto loves his job as a television presenter. When people ask him why, he has an immediate and definite answer – it's never boring! There are disadvantages, of course, as there are with any job – he works very long hours and there's always the pressure of having to look good on television – but he loves all that. He just wishes the salary were higher!

   A Roberto is glad that television presenters work at regular times.
   B Roberto is satisfied that television presenters are paid well.
   C Roberto is certain that a television presenter's job is always interesting.

2 When Agnes was at school, she had lots of ideas about what she could do as a career but few of them seemed realistic. She was good at maths but not much else and her teachers thought she should become an accountant. That didn't seem like a good plan to her because her hobby was playing computer games and designing those seemed like more fun. Her parents weren't keen on that career for her, though.

   A Agnes wanted to do what her teachers said.
   B Agnes did well in different subjects at school.
   C Agnes liked the idea of designing computer games.

3 Max was really worried about getting everything ready for the party before all the guests arrived in two hours' time. He was starting to think it had been a mistake to invite a large number of friends all at the same time! The food was ready to be cooked on the barbecue but he still needed to decorate the garden, which was where everyone would sit. Luckily, it wasn't going to rain so he didn't need to think about putting up umbrellas!

   A Max was excited about so many people coming to his party.
   B Max was looking forward to having a party in his garden.
   C Max was relieved about the weather conditions.

4 I had never thought of trying to run a marathon but when one of my friends decided to give it a go, I thought 'Why not? How difficult can it be?' How wrong I was! I did six months' hard training and completely changed my diet so that I would become stronger. It wasn't easy at all! I was sure that I would be nervous on the day of the marathon itself but I knew that I had prepared well. And in the end I enjoyed it, even though I took more than four hours to finish!

   A The writer was happy with the preparation she did for the marathon.
   B The writer expected running the marathon to be difficult.
   C The writer's friend convinced her to run a marathon.

Identifying the writer's purpose

> **TIP:** A writer usually has a purpose for writing an article or a letter.

6 **Match the sentences 1–10 with the writer's purpose A–J.**

1 I think we should meet at the cinema on Saturday.
2 The best thing is for you to take the job.
3 You should go and see the film – it's great!
4 Why don't you come here for lunch tomorrow?
5 It was fun as it was hot and the beach was wonderful!
6 The ticket was expensive and the view was terrible!
7 Don't forget to buy some milk on your way home.
8 The house is red with a yellow roof.
9 Would you like me to cook the meal for you?
10 I'm sorry I was late yesterday.

A to explain why they enjoyed a day out
B to recommend a film
C to complain about the cost of something
D to suggest an arrangement
E to remind someone to do something
F to offer to help someone
G to describe something
H to give someone advice about work
I to apologise for something
J to invite someone for a meal

7 **Look at the paragraphs below. What is the writer doing in each one? Choose A or B.**

1 I was really looking forward to the trip to the Arctic because I had always wanted to go there. You can imagine my disappointment when it was cancelled because of bad weather! I can understand the reasons but no one from the tour company got in touch to explain what was going to happen about rearranging the trip or a refund. I didn't like that at all.

A describing a disappointing holiday
B complaining about bad service

2 The art gallery was really interesting, with interactive exhibits as well as the more usual paintings on the walls. My personal favourite was the lady with her horse, which you could move through computer graphics. It's a fun gallery to visit, especially for children, and well worth an afternoon's visit for the whole family.

A recommending a gallery
B reminding people about an exhibition

3 You came to my house last week and you were coming again tomorrow, but how about meeting in town instead? I've got to buy a present for my sister so you could help me with that. Then we could have lunch at that new restaurant. What do you think?

A inviting someone to lunch
B suggesting a different arrangement

4 It was fun meeting yesterday and it was a shame that the traffic was so bad that I missed the first part of the film. I hope it didn't spoil the afternoon for you – I'll set off earlier next time!

A explaining why the writer made a mistake
B expressing regret about the afternoon

5 Hi, Janie! I'm really looking forward to seeing you next week. I've made lots of plans for us and we'll have a great time! Shall I meet you at the station when you arrive? That'll be better than you taking a taxi. Let me know!

A making Janie an offer
B giving Janie advice

6 Hi, Mo! I hope you had fun on your birthday and I'm sorry that I couldn't make it to the party in the evening. It was impossible for me to change the meeting at work, so I'm sure that you understand. I'll see you on Saturday as planned, anyway, and we can have our own small celebration then.

A apologising for missing Mo's party
B changing an arrangement with Mo

For each question, choose the correct answer.

My snowboarding experiences

Young snowboarder Maya Gonzales writes about her experiences.

I've always loved excitement and my parents encouraged me to try to be the best at everything I did. I started gymnastics when I was three and was winning competitions when I was six. By the time I was fourteen, I was finding it too easy. Doing the same routines was becoming boring and I needed a change. My family used to go skiing every year, so I could ski almost as soon as I could walk! So I convinced my parents to let me try snowboarding, which I thought looked harder than skiing. How right I was!

The first step was managing the board – it's not as easy as you might think. I felt I had lost control over my body and every time I fell over it was difficult to stand up again. In fact, I was sure that everyone was laughing at me, which wasn't a good feeling! But I had a good instructor and, once I learnt how to balance, I improved quickly. He said that my previous gymnastics classes helped me with that. Then I discovered there were tricks I could do on my snowboard. I decided I wanted to spend the winter learning to do these properly.

The first competition I entered was a real surprise. I was used to being a winner but this was a completely different experience. The standard was really high, which was a shock, and I was very nervous. Then one of the other competitors told me I had the talent to get to the top, although he didn't tell me how to do it. What he said made me feel more positive and although I only came tenth, it felt more like a small success. He also said he wasn't as good as me, which was kind of him!

Now I'm more confident, my aim is to win a national competition. I've got a new coach and I'm working on new tricks that really challenge me – they're often dangerous, but I love trying them. I know I have to take chances if I want to be the best. I really hope I can inspire other people to try it. It's a great sport and you'll have lots of fun, even if you don't ever do it in competitions!

1   Why did Maya decide to learn how to snowboard?

    A   to try something dangerous

    B   to overcome a fear

    C   to face a new challenge

    D   to please her parents

2   How did Maya feel when she started snowboarding?

    A   keen to learn more about it

    B   embarrassed about her lack of ability

    C   grateful for her gymnastics knowledge

    D   worried about getting injured

3   Maya says that a snowboarder who talked to her at her first competition

    A   gave her some good advice.

    B   made her feel better about the result.

    C   encouraged her to change her sport.

    D   showed her new moves to work on.

4   What is Maya doing in the final paragraph?

    A   recommending the sport to other people

    B   describing how she does her training

    C   explaining why she wants to be successful

    D   outlining ways of making the sport more popular

5   What might Maya say about learning to snowboard?

    A   I'm starting to lose that feeling of excitement when I snowboard and I worry if there are other competitors who are really good.

    B   I knew exactly what would happen when I took part in my first competition, and I enjoyed it.

    C   I'm amazed I've been chosen to take part in the National Championships, especially as I've been dreaming of it since I was young.

    D   I don't get as anxious before competitions as I used to and I'm hoping to perform the tricks I'm learning at an important competition soon.

TEST

- In Reading Part 4, you read one long text. This may be about a person or an event.
- There are five sentences missing from the text.
- There are eight sentences (A–H) opposite the text. You choose which sentence fits each of the five gaps.

- You can only use a sentence once and there are three sentences you don't need to use.
- You need to think about how the text is organised and how ideas in it are linked together.
- There is one mark for each correct answer.

Practice task

1 Four sentences have been removed from the text below. For each question, choose the correct answer. There are three extra sentences which you do not need to use.

Antarctica: The final frontier?

While nomads have always travelled from one place to another as a way of life, explorers have challenged themselves to reach isolated parts of the planet, and even beyond into space. But there's one place that remains largely untouched and that's Antarctica. There's one obvious explanation for this. **(1)** _____ That's when the sea ice melts. There aren't any towns or even small villages – just a few empty houses left over from old expeditions and some more modern buildings where scientists do research into things like climate change.

Although it's hard to find people in Antarctica, it's certainly not difficult to find other living creatures. **(2)** _____ It may be difficult to see them, though, as the snowy landscape seems to go on forever.

Apart from the cold, what you'll notice first is the silence. **(3)** _____ Some people find it too quiet! Travelling is pretty difficult even for those in search of adventure. There aren't any roads or marked routes. Instead, huge mountains reach high into the sky and enormous icebergs the size of skyscrapers float on the icy water.

Strangely, for such a cold place, scientists have discovered many volcanoes in Antarctica. In fact, there may be 91 of them under the ice. **(4)** _____ With so much to find out about the continent, it remains a fascinating place. More and more tourists are keen to see it for themselves, which could be a problem in this beautiful area of the planet.

A So for that reason it's difficult to explain how cold it is there.

B It's not like anything you'll hear anywhere else.

C There's a vast range of wildlife there, including whales, penguins and birds.

D The best way to travel there is by boat.

E People can only get there in spring when temperatures rise a little.

F This is why it's expensive for tourists to visit the area.

G More research is needed to discover whether any of these are active, though.

How did you do?

2 Check your answers.

3 Look again at extracts from the text in Ex 1 with the missing sentences in place. Look at the words in bold. What do they refer to?

1 But there's one place that remains largely untouched and that's Antarctica. There's one obvious explanation for this. People can only get **there** in spring when temperatures rise a little. **That's when** the sea ice melts.

2 Although it's hard to find people in Antarctica, it's certainly not difficult to find other living creatures. There's a vast range of wildlife **there**, including whales, penguins and birds. It may be difficult to see **them**, though, as the snowy landscape seems to go on forever.

3 Apart from the cold, what you'll notice first is the silence. **It**'s not like anything you'll hear anywhere else. Some people find **it** too quiet!

4 Strangely, for such a cold place, scientists have discovered many volcanoes in Antarctica. In fact, there may be 91 of **them** under the ice. More research is needed to discover whether any of **these** are active, though.

Strategies and skills

Pronoun references

> **TIP:** Think carefully about pronouns and what they can refer to.

Pronouns can refer back to words or ideas already mentioned or can refer forwards to ideas that are mentioned later.

1 **What do the pronouns in bold refer to? For each question, choose A or B.**

1 Some of my friends are doing part-time jobs in cafés. None of **them** are having much fun, though.
A my friends   B cafés

2 My mother advised me to work in another country for a short time. That's what she did **herself** when she was young.
A my mother   B me

3 I had a holiday in France last year. **It** was wonderful because the resort was such a beautiful place.
A the resort   B the holiday

4 I'd love to visit Australia but it's a problem getting **there** because the flight is so long.
A the flight   B Australia

5 Although **this** may change in the future, it's surprising how cheap international travel is at the moment!
A how cheap international   B the future
travel is

6 Although I can't afford to rent any of **them**, I'd still love to live in one of the apartments with views of the river.
A views of the river   B the apartments

7 My teacher advised me to study music but I wasn't sure I wanted to do **that**. I didn't think I was good enough.
A I wasn't good enough   B study music

8 A friend I hadn't seen for years phoned me last night. **This** was a lovely surprise!
A my friend's phone call   B an old school friend

2 **Complete the sentences with the pronouns in the box.**

> her   here   it   them   there   these   they   this

1 I hadn't been _____ before so it took me ages to find the restaurant.

2 I always post blogs whenever I travel and my friends like reading _____ .

3 My sister was good at maths and so I asked _____ for help.

4 Our week at the beach was great fun and all the family loved _____ .

5 Although _____ were expensive, we decided to get tickets for the concert anyway.

6 You can see foxes in cities, although wild animals like _____ can be quite shy.

7 Many students learn new vocabulary by heart and _____ is something they find useful.

8 We've been standing _____ for ages and there's no sign of the bus!

3 **Read the extracts. For each question, choose the correct answer, A, B or C.**

1 I felt very worried about moving to a new city because I thought I might not make friends, I might be lonely and I would probably keep getting lost. **It** was completely unnecessary! I made many friends, wasn't lonely and never got lost!
'It' refers to
A feeling very worried.
B moving to the new city.
C making friends.

2 Nowadays, everyone has a mobile phone, which they use absolutely everywhere. For example, people often text as they walk along the road, even though **this** can be a dangerous thing to do!
'this' refers to
A using a phone everywhere.
B texting while walking.
C walking along the road.

3 'Can you tell me how to get to the station, please?' I asked a man at the bus stop.
'Go to the corner and turn left at the bank. You can't miss **it**!' he answered.
'it' refers to
A the bank.
B the corner.
C the station.

4 I love going to watch my local football team play, although the fans can sometimes be rather loud. **That**'s not a problem for me when my team scores a goal, though!
'That' refers to
A scoring a goal.
B the noise fans make.
C watching the local team.

4 One of the sentences (A or B) can follow each short extract. Use the pronouns and reference words to help you choose the correct one.

1 Dancing is an activity that lots of people enjoy. The combination of music and movement brings happiness not only to the dancers but also to anyone watching their performance.
   A Their hobby is popular with people of all ages.
   B It's a very special thing for everyone to experience.

2 People understand two things about keeping fit – that you have to do regular exercise and that it's also important to eat healthy food.
   A Both of these things are good and have equal benefits.
   B Their ideas have positive benefits, including staying fit and healthy.

3 It's said that Christopher Columbus first brought cocoa beans back to Europe between 1502 and 1504, but it was Joseph Fry in 1847 who discovered that he could mix cacao butter with Dutch cocoa and make bars of chocolate.
   A This was the start of the chocolate bar as we know it today.
   B This one became popular in England very quickly.

4 Although not everyone realises this, in some places cross-country skiing is more popular than other more extreme winter sports, for a variety of reasons.
   A It's something you can't do without a teacher.
   B It's cheaper, safer and you don't need a mountain to do it.

5 My sister heard nothing from the company until three weeks after her job interview. Then she received a letter.
   A It said she had got the job and could start the following week.
   B She thought about calling the company to ask whether she had got the job.

6 The resort had lots of things to do, such as swimming, canoeing and rock climbing.
   A We tried all these during our stay there and had a great time.
   B It was a very big place, which we rather liked.

SPEAKING BOOST

Discuss or answer.

1 Describe a travel experience that you would like to have.
2 What films or television programmes have you seen about a journey or an expedition?

General points and supporting information

> **TIP:** Writers sometimes give an example to show what they mean or to explain something like an opinion more clearly.

5 For each extract, choose the correct linking phrase. Is the text after the linking phrase giving an example or explaining an opinion?

1 I worked in the leisure centre for three months but I knew after the first week that it wasn't the right job for me because there were some things I didn't like. **Obviously, / For example,** I hated working at the weekends even though I had nothing else to do then.

   example / opinion

2 Different things can change how we feel, **like / in other words,** music can make us feel happy or sad. Jazz always makes me happy!

   example / opinion

3 We're encouraged to think about the environment more and not drive our cars on short journeys. **Fortunately, / Clearly,** there's a great bus service where I live so it's not a problem.

   example / opinion

4 Ice cream can be good for us! Although it does contain cream and sugar, which aren't healthy. **Luckily, / Unfortunately,** it does still give us calcium and vitamins, so if that's true, it means I can eat lots of it!

   example / opinion

5 The weather changes my mood – if it's raining, I feel sad. **I'm lucky / I'm unhappy** to live in a place where it doesn't rain very often!

   example / opinion

6 I don't really like studying in the evenings because I feel tired then. **So what I do is / So it's surprising that** I get up early and study before breakfast. That works for me.

   example / opinion

Some sentences add more information to what has gone before and others introduce a new idea which is connected to the previous sentence.

6 Decide which sentence (A–F) follows each of the sentences 1–6. Does each one add more information or introduce a new idea?

1 He's a very talented singer who became famous after winning a competition on television.

2 Most of the hotel was very modern, with a new swimming pool and restaurant.

3 Some people feel depressed in the winter when it's cold.

4 People can lead unhealthy working lives.

5 I feel very optimistic about the future.

6 When I travel by plane I always feel nervous.

A They might work very long hours and not see their family very much.

B I don't mind travelling by boat though. In fact, I find it quite relaxing.

C It's interesting that many people who come second in such competitions go on to be more successful than the actual winner.

D Unfortunately, the bedrooms were still rather old.

E That's because I'm sure we'll solve the climate problems, because scientists are working hard on it.

F Most people when asked would probably say that spring or summer is their favourite time of year, when temperatures are warmer and the days are longer.

Checking text coherence

TIP: When you have chosen the sentences for the exam task, read the whole text again to check that it makes sense.

7 A student has done this short task but has chosen the wrong answers from the options A–F. What has the student done wrong? What are the correct answers?

Working as a **stage manager**

I love the theatre. I've wanted to be an actor since I was a child but sadly I just wasn't good enough. I did try and went to drama school for several years, but my teachers were honest with me. **(1)** _B_ I was upset about this at first and thought I would have to give up my dreams. Then someone suggested becoming a stage manager. **(2)** _D_ I investigated and it looked perfect for me.

So what does a stage manager do? Everything! Obviously, I'm not on the stage, though – I'm the most important person behind the scenes. **(3)** _C_ To do this, I need to know about everything that happens in your theatre. I have to be good at communication, organisation and solving problems. I also have to do practical things in the theatre. **(4)** _A_ If anything goes wrong, then it's my job to fix it. I always have to be ready for surprises!

A stage manager must be good with people and enjoy working with others, which I do. But for me, the best part of the job is the excitement I've always felt about being in a theatre – I love it.

A It's a job that pays well.

B I didn't know what this was.

C For example, I've cleaned the stage, made costumes and put up scenery.

D I knew that I couldn't make it my career.

E There are lots of things that actors do, too.

F I make sure that everything goes well.

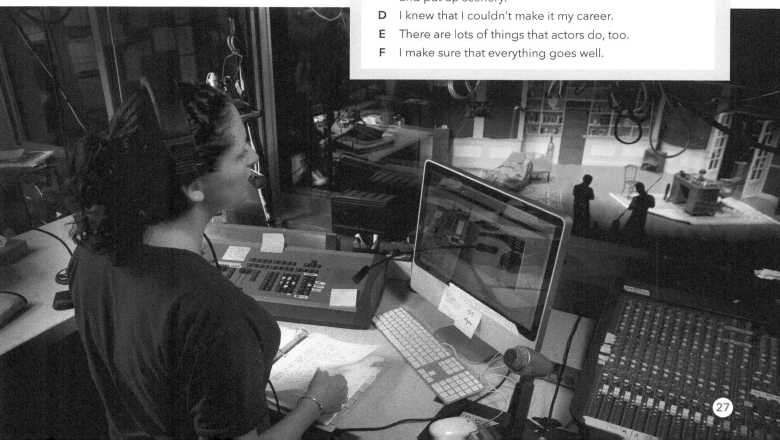

Five sentences have been removed from the text below. For each question, choose the correct answer. There are three extra sentences which you do not need to use.

A pilot's life

I always knew I wanted to be a pilot so as soon as I finished school I started applying to different airlines to join their training courses. I was offered an interview with two different companies. **(1)** _____ Luckily, I did much better the next time and the company accepted me. There was a lot to learn on the course and it was more stressful than I expected, but I enjoyed it.

After years of training and studying, I'm now qualified as a professional pilot and the job has lots of advantages. **(2)** _____ I've been to hundreds of interesting places and I often stay in some of them for a couple of days between flights. In spite of that, though, there are some negatives. If I'm in an amazing place, there's no one to share it with. Also, if I go to the same place regularly, it gets boring.

My job affects my social life, too. My working days aren't fixed, which means I'm often free during the week when my friends or family are busy at college or work. **(3)** _____ It's not all bad, though, because it does mean that I have the opportunity to develop new interests.

Surprisingly, the lack of routine can have unexpected consequences. It means I have to make a special effort to take care of myself. **(4)** _____ Organising that can be difficult when I'm travelling so I always make sure any hotel I stay in has a pool or gym.

Do I regret anything? I wish I had more qualifications that are not connected with flying. **(5)** _____ Because of that I'm now taking an online business course in my free time but it's hard to fit everything in. I do know I'm lucky, though, and I have a dream job!

A There will certainly be other destinations to explore after that.

E That's why I eat healthy food and do exercise like running.

B That's no fun because I have to do stuff on my own!

F The most obvious of these is travelling all over the world.

C Unfortunately, I was nervous and did badly in the first one!

G They would give me opportunities for a new career when I stop flying.

D It generally surprises people when they discover how long it takes.

H That's a difficult journey to describe to other people.

ABOUT THE TASK

- In Reading Part 5, you read one short text. Six words are missing from the text.

- There are four possible options (A, B, C and D) for you to choose from to fill each gap.

- The gaps test your understanding of vocabulary and collocation.

- There is one mark for each correct answer.

Practice task

1 Read the first paragraph of a text about a visit to some waterfalls in South America. For each question, choose the correct answer.

My visit to
Iguazu waterfalls

When I went on a trip to South America I was looking **(1)** _____ to seeing the Iguazu waterfalls because I had heard how amazing they were. When we got there, the noise of the water was incredible! My friends wanted to ride the small boat which took visitors up to the biggest fall. The captain gave us special waterproof clothes to **(2)** _____ on because he said we would get very wet. I'm **(3)** _____ on having exciting experiences but as we got closer to the falls the noise of the water was frightening. We had to shout to each other! Some people were trying to take photos but I could only hold on tight to the boat. The trip only **(4)** _____ a short time but I was happy when it was over!

1	A forward	B ahead	C through	D advance
2	A get	B work	C put	D carry
3	A fond	B keen	C interested	D fascinated
4	A went	B made	C kept	D lasted

How did you do?

2 Check your answers.

3 Look at the four answers again. Which one is

A a verb?

B an adjective followed by a preposition?

C part of a phrasal verb?

D part of a fixed phrase?

4 Look again at the options that were wrong in Ex 1 questions 1–4. Choose the correct option to complete each of the sentences below.

1 A I looked _____ the kitchen window and saw the postman standing outside.

   B The small boat went _____ of all the other larger boats.

   C I booked my train tickets well in _____ of my trip.

2 A I want to _____ on in life and make money so I work hard now.

   B I need to _____ on my English grammar to improve it – it's not very good.

   C I'm going to _____ on playing for the football team even though my friends have given it up.

3 A My brother is _____ by science fiction and would love to go into space.

   B I'm very _____ of travelling – I do it whenever I can.

   C My sister is _____ in history and often goes to museums.

4 A I _____ an effort to study harder and so I passed my exam.

   B I _____ to Spain last year on holiday and really enjoyed it.

   C I _____ making mistakes in spelling so my teacher gave me extra lessons.

Strategies and skills

Verb phrases

> **TIP:** When you learn a new verb, learn the words it can be used with.

The same verb can be used in many different phrases but it may have a different meaning.

1 **Complete the sentences with the verbs in the box. Use each verb twice.**

> come   do   hold   make   take

1 It's good to _____ a favour for a friend and help them when they need it.

2 It took me ages to _____ a decision about which car to buy.

3 I'm going to try to _____ my best in the interview because I really want the job!

4 It's good to _____ a chance sometimes and not worry too much about it.

5 I hope your dreams will _____ true and you'll be successful in your new career.

6 People often _____ mistakes with grammar when they start to learn a new language.

7 The tennis club is going to _____ a competition for new players.

8 The concert will _____ place on Saturday in the football stadium.

9 I was so pleased that I didn't _____ last in the race!

10 Everyone should _____ on tightly if they have to stand up on a moving train.

Discuss or answer.

1 In what situations do you listen to music on your own? In what situations do you listen with friends?

2 Are there any sounds that you dislike? Give examples.

Prepositional phrases

> **TIP:** Always read the words after the gap carefully. There may be a preposition that helps you choose the right option.

2 **Read the sentences and look at the highlighted prepositions. Choose the word that goes in front of each preposition.**

1 I'm very **pleased / satisfied / proud** of my new flat.

2 I sometimes feel **nervous / frightened / worried** of a thunderstorm, which is silly!

3 I often make nice pasta but I'm not very **good / curious / fond** at cooking other things.

4 I'm **fascinated / interested / keen** in science fiction.

5 I'd never **seen / noticed / heard** of this book before but it's really exciting to read.

6 I don't mind what we do this evening – it **depends / goes / decides** on what you want to do.

7 He's always **talking / saying / informing** about his new house.

8 My home town is **beautiful / famous / different** for the big castle on the hill.

9 I'm **satisfied / excited / interested** with the way I played in the match last week!

10 I was **disappointed / sad / miserable** with the film – I wish I hadn't gone to see it.

> **TIP:** The preposition may sometimes come in front of a gap.

3 **Complete the sentences with the prepositions in the box.**

> at   by   for   in (x2)   of   on   to

1 _____ be honest, I actually enjoyed the film.

2 I love going _____ holiday in the summer.

3 I often get up late so I'm usually _____ a hurry to catch the bus.

4 My sister once left the oven on for hours _____ mistake. It could have been dangerous!

5 I enjoy spending time _____ home because I can relax there.

6 I often choose to eat fish and chips _____ lunch – it gives me energy.

7 It's a good idea to take some warm clothes when you go on holiday, but _____ course you may not need them!

8 I don't know him very well – _____ fact, I didn't meet him until recently.

4 Match the sentence beginnings (1–6) with the endings (A–F).

1 It was really exciting to meet the actor in
2 My brother was so tired
3 When I met my new colleague, we had a lot in
4 I was impressed he could learn vocabulary by
5 My sister was worried
6 It's so typical

A common and got on really well.
B of my cousin to arrive late!
C person, but sadly she wasn't very friendly.
D about taking her driving test, but she passed it first time.
E of studying that he decided to leave college and get a job.
F heart so easily because I find it difficult.

5 Correct the mistakes with the prepositions in bold.

1 The view from my room in the hotel is similar **from** my friend's.
2 My friends always complain **at** the food there – I don't know why they don't go to a different restaurant!
3 I lent my book **for** a friend but he forgot to give it back.
4 The manager apologised **in** the long delay with our order.
5 Have you ever argued with your friends **for** politics?
6 Whenever I go to a sports event there's always a tall person standing **on** front of me!

Verbs related to clothes and other verb collocations

TIP: It's helpful to learn words in topic areas.

6 Complete the sentences with the words in the boxes. You may need to change the form of some of the words and there is one extra word in each box that you do not need.

Clothes

> fit hang iron match suit try

1 I want my clothes to _____ well because if they're too big or too small they look terrible.
2 I hate _____ clothes – I have better things to do with my time!
3 I never wear black – the colour doesn't _____ me at all.
4 I always _____ my clothes in the wardrobe when I take them off at night.
5 People look smart when their clothes _____ – if all the colours are different they don't look nice.

Work

> attend do leave put take work

6 When you're at work, it's important to _____ regular breaks.
7 Many students _____ part-time when they're at college.
8 I'm sure I can _____ my new job well – I feel very confident about it.
9 I have to _____ a meeting with my manager first thing on Monday morning.
10 I try to _____ the office early on a Friday afternoon if I can.

Sport

> compete do enjoy go join keep

11 I try to _____ fit by running three times a week.
12 It's hard to find enough time to _____ exercise regularly.
13 I'd love to _____ a hockey club but I don't think I'm good enough.
14 My friend wants me to _____ swimming with her but I hate cold water!
15 It's good for children to _____ against each other in sports competitions at school.

Entertainment and free time

> browse download have play record stream

16 I'd love to be able to _____ a musical instrument, but I can't.
17 There are apps you can _____ connected with any hobby.
18 Most people I know have stopped buying CDs because they _____ music instead.
19 Everyone should _____ a hobby that they can do to relax. Mine's playing computer games!
20 Most people waste a lot of time _____ the internet – I know I do.

Education

> do follow get make pass study

21 I wish I had _____ another language at school but I only did English.
22 It's important to me to _____ this exam otherwise I can't go to college.
23 The worst thing about my course is how much extra research I need to _____ . I'm always in the library.
24 I'm hoping to _____ a good qualification at the end of my course.
25 I always _____ notes in lectures so that I can remember the main points.

Daily activities

> brush   catch   follow   have   make   put

26   It's easier to manage the working week if you have a routine to _____ .

27   I get up early to _____ a bus to college at seven o'clock.

28   I always _____ my bed before I leave home in the morning,

29   I can't imagine leaving home without _____ my teeth!

30   One of the most relaxing things is _____ a shower before going to bed.

Discuss or answer.

1   What's your favourite item of clothing and your favourite pair of shoes? Why are they your favourite?

2   Describe a recent shopping experience.

Easily confused words

TIP: Some words have similar meanings and are easy to confuse. Think about the exact meaning of each word, how it is used and any prepositions or collocations it has.

7 **Choose the correct word to complete the sentences.**

1   You can see beautiful **scenery / nature** in the mountains but it can be dangerous when the weather changes.

2   Please **remind / remember** your scarf when you go out – it's cold today.

3   In my **opinion / idea**, people don't think about the environment enough.

4   Why don't you **come / go** round to my house tonight and have a meal with me?

5   Can I **borrow / lend** your umbrella, please? It's raining.

6   I never know where my car keys are – I'm always **losing / missing** them!

7   It'd be great to **work / job** for an international company – I'd like to work abroad one day.

8   The train **travel / journey** from Cambridge to London doesn't take long.

8 **Choose the correct word (A-D) to complete each sentence.**

1   The _____ from my seat in the stadium wasn't very good.
   A scene   **B** view   **C** sight   **D** look

2   If you _____ fruit in the fridge, it usually lasts longer.
   A keep   **B** hold   **C** carry   **D** get

3   My friends are always taking photos of things they're doing and _____ them online.
   A sending   **B** posting   **C** giving   **D** delivering

4   The singer _____ her first album in 2016 when she was only 15.
   A brought   **B** displayed   **C** recorded   **D** presented

5   The teacher _____ the students about the homework she wanted them to do.
   A told   **B** said   **C** explained   **D** described

6   London is a popular _____ for tourists from all over the world.
   A travel   **B** trip   **C** excursion   **D** destination

7   The first reliable _____ records of the castle appeared in the tenth century.
   A old   **B** historical   **C** antique   **D** past

8   It's easier to travel by plane if you only _____ hand luggage on board with you.
   A fetch   **B** lift   **C** take   **D** bring

Phrasal verbs

The missing word may be part of a phrasal verb. You may be given verbs or prepositions to choose from.

9 **Choose the correct word (A-D) to complete the phrasal verb in each sentence.**

1   The last thing I do before I go to sleep is _____ off the light.
   A switch   **B** get   **C** go   **D** make

2   I hate buying clothes online because I can't _____ them on before I buy them.
   A do   **B** get   **C** try   **D** keep

3   I always try to think _____ a problem carefully before deciding what to do.
   A on   **B** at   **C** about   **D** for

4   Whenever our neighbour goes on holiday, we look _____ their cat.
   A for   **B** after   **C** out   **D** about

5   I want to try a new sport, so I am going to take _____ hockey.
   A down   **B** on   **C** about   **D** up

6   It's important to me to _____ everything away in the right place so that the flat is tidy.
   A get   **B** put   **C** take   **D** carry

7   The meeting _____ on until the evening – I found it very tiring!
   A went   **B** moved   **C** got   **D** took

8   I have given _____ playing in tennis competitions because I don't have time to practise.
   A in   **B** on   **C** up   **D** through

For each question, choose the correct answer.

Indoor skydiving

Have you ever wanted to try skydiving but felt too scared to do it? If you can't bring yourself to jump out of a plane but still **(1)** _____ about trying it, then indoor skydiving may be the answer.

Although it **(2)** _____ the name of the extreme sport, indoor skydiving isn't really the same. You go into a wind tunnel which creates conditions you might experience if you jump out of a plane but because this activity is done under carefully controlled conditions, it's safe for anyone who wants to **(3)** _____ part. You wear special clothes including goggles and a helmet, and ear plugs because it's noisy inside the tunnel. One benefit of being indoors is that the weather can't **(4)** _____ any problems!

An instructor **(5)** _____ after you on your first flight but then you can start to fly with less help while still being safe. I felt very **(6)** _____ of myself after I flew! It's a worldwide sport which is safe but exciting for people of all ages.

1	A	imagine	B	create	C	hope	D	dream
2	A	combines	B	shares	C	mixes	D	gives
3	A	keep	B	bring	C	take	D	get
4	A	cause	B	make	C	have	D	begin
5	A	sees	B	looks	C	works	D	helps
6	A	pleased	B	satisfied	C	happy	D	proud

- In Reading Part 6, you read one short text. Six words are missing from the text.
- You have to decide on the correct word to fill each gap and you write this word in the gap.

- The gaps test your understanding of grammatical words such as prepositions, pronouns, articles, auxiliary verbs, question words and so on.
- You must spell the word you write correctly.
- There is one mark for each correct answer.

Practice task

1 Read the first paragraph of a text about daydreaming. For each question, write the correct answer. Write one word for each gap.

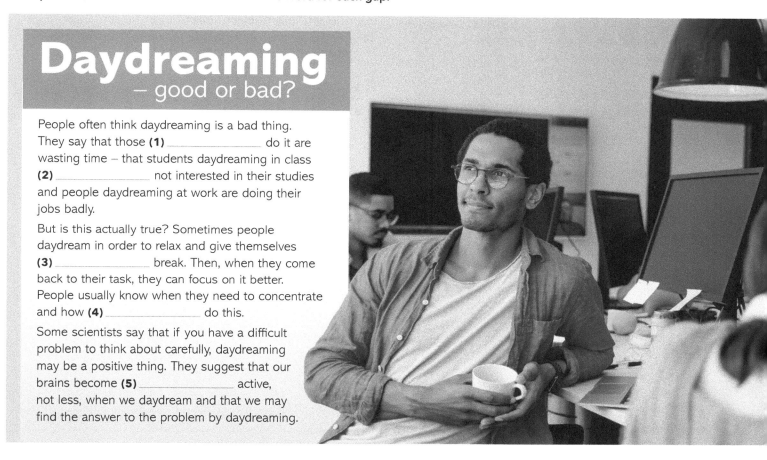

Daydreaming
– good or bad?

People often think daydreaming is a bad thing. They say that those **(1)** _____ do it are wasting time – that students daydreaming in class **(2)** _____ not interested in their studies and people daydreaming at work are doing their jobs badly.

But is this actually true? Sometimes people daydream in order to relax and give themselves **(3)** _____ break. Then, when they come back to their task, they can focus on it better. People usually know when they need to concentrate and how **(4)** _____ do this.

Some scientists say that if you have a difficult problem to think about carefully, daydreaming may be a positive thing. They suggest that our brains become **(5)** _____ active, not less, when we daydream and that we may find the answer to the problem by daydreaming.

How did you do?

2 Check your answers.

3 Look at the answers you wrote in the gaps (1–5) in Ex 1 again. Which answer is

A   part of a verb?

B   a relative pronoun?

C   part of a comparative?

D   an indefinite article?

E   part of an infinitive?

TEACH

Strategies and skills
Relative clauses

1 **Complete the sentences with the relative pronouns in the box.**

> that   what   where   when   which   who
> whose   why

1 I live in a small village _____ everyone knows each other.

2 My sister is a person _____ loves to play tennis.

3 I have no idea _____ to do on Saturday now that my friend isn't coming to stay.

4 We were late so the show had already started _____ we arrived.

5 During the course I studied with Joe, a teacher _____ special interest is ancient history.

6 I wasn't sure _____ the tour was cancelled and no one could tell me the reason.

7 The hotel, _____ was located in the town centre, was fantastic.

8 The show _____ I had originally intended to see was sold out so I couldn't get tickets.

SPEAKING BOOST

Discuss or answer.

1 What time do you usually go to bed? Is it the same in the week as at weekends?

2 In what situations do you find it difficult to get to sleep? What can you do to help?

Articles and quantifiers

2 **Complete the paragraph with *a*, *an* or *the*.**

My country life

When I woke up it was very early in **(1)** _____ morning. I got out of bed, went to **(2)** _____ kitchen and made myself **(3)** _____ cup of coffee. It was going to be **(4)** _____ very hot day and I could hear birds singing in **(5)** _____ trees outside my window. I love living in **(6)** _____ countryside, even though I have fewer opportunities for entertainment. I used to enjoy **(7)** _____ evening out with friends, though now I think it's more of **(8)** _____ advantage to be able to do things like walking and cycling! I think I'm **(9)** _____ healthiest I've ever been and don't regret **(10)** _____ thing about moving here.

3 **Choose the correct word to complete each sentence.**

1 We had to run because we didn't have **many** / **much** time before the bus came.

2 I only have a **little** / **few** work to do this weekend so we can go to the beach.

3 I don't think that **many** / **few** people are coming to the party.

4 I need to get **some** / **any** bread next time I go to the supermarket – we don't have **any** / **many** in the cupboard.

5 Only a **few** / **little** students get the top grade.

6 The jewellery she buys can cost as **much** / **many** as £2,000, which is a **lot** / **lots** of money!

7 I've lost my purse so I haven't got **any** / **some** cash on me. Can you lend me **some** / **lots**?

8 I find grammar a **little** / **much** difficult so I try to do a **few** / **many** exercises every night.

Comparing

4 **Rewrite each sentence with the word in brackets in the correct place.**

1 Jodie wears smart clothes that she always looks elegant. (such)
_____

2 Most sports cars are expensive for people like me to buy. (too)
_____

3 I'm not hungry to eat a big meal at the moment. (enough)
_____

4 The tram was crowded that I had to walk home. (so)
_____

5 The second film was as good as the first one, in my opinion. (not)
_____

6 The important thing for me is to do well at college. (most)
_____

7 Some people think that dogs are friendly than cats. (more)
_____

8 I haven't finished my project yet – it's harder I thought. (than)
_____

5 **Match the sentence beginnings (1–8) with the endings (A–H).**

1 I was so busy reading

2 I didn't realise that there would be so

3 The hotter the day,

4 Jose is now one of the world's

5 I love the film – I've seen it

6 I didn't know how difficult

7 I was cold walking home because it was

8 The job would be perfect for someone

A like my friend Elena.

B that I missed my station.

C most popular actors.

D such a snowy day.

E the course would be.

F the more difficult it is to stay cool.

G more than ten times.

H many people at the concert.

6 Complete the paragraph with the words in the box.

> as   less   like   most   same   such   than   the

Do people think like
computers?

Many studies have been done on whether computers can think in the **(1)** _____ way as people. But do people ever think like computers?

Computers are obviously **(2)** _____ best at some things, **(3)** _____ as maths or remembering information, but they are **(4)** _____ skilful at identifying objects. The **(5)** _____ difficult thing for them is that they can only recognise what they have been programmed to see. So for example, if little changes are made to a picture of a car so that it looks **(6)** _____ something else, the computer can no longer recognise it.

It's easy to think that people would not make the same mistake and would do better **(7)** _____ the computer but strangely, when a group of people were shown the same picture they were as bad **(8)** _____ the computer.

Linking words and expressions

TIP: Read the whole sentence before you choose the linking word.

8 Choose the correct word (A, B or C) to complete each sentence.

1 _____ travelling by bus can be slow, it's good for the environment.
   A Although   B But   C However

2 I wasn't keen to go to the festival _____ the tickets were so expensive.
   A unless   B because   C whereas

3 We took my friend to the castle _____ she could see the paintings there.
   A so that   B since   C where

4 The winter is really cold here _____ the summers are hot.
   A if   B when   C but

5 There is a weekly market where you can buy fruit and vegetables, _____ .
   A after   B and   C too

6 We chatted to each other _____ we were waiting in the queue.
   A while   B unless   C for

Discuss or answer.

1 In a typical day, what do you use a mobile phone, laptop and/or tablet for?

2 Have you ever lost a mobile phone, laptop or other piece of technology? What happened?

Future forms

7 Find and correct the mistakes with future forms in the sentences. Two sentences are correct.

1 Harry is going have his hair cut tomorrow.

2 Violet has decided she won't doing the college course next year.

3 I don't feel well so I think I'll go home now.

4 I was going to cook but I think I'll to get a takeaway instead.

5 I promise I'll being there on time tomorrow!

6 I going to study tonight so I can't come to the cinema after all.

7 The train leaves at ten o'clock so don't be late!

8 I'll helping you with your computer problem if you like.

For each question, write the correct answer. Write one word for each gap.

Why are extreme sports popular?

Extreme sports like free climbing or big wave surfing seem to be thrilling and, in comparison, more traditional sports **(1)** _____ as golf or tennis may seem rather boring. But why are they becoming so popular?

The reason seems obvious – people want excitement and some find this by doing extreme leisure activities like bungee jumping. But this explanation is not **(2)** _____ whole truth for people who take extreme sports very seriously. These people are real athletes **(3)** _____ train hard, prepare well and are experts in their chosen sport.

So **(4)** _____ is the explanation for the increasing interest in extreme sports? Solo rock climbers speak **(5)** _____ using all their senses as they climb – hearing every tiny sound and feeling every movement around them. They describe it as an unusual and positive experience. So it's **(6)** _____ the excitement or the danger that makes them do it but the feeling of being alive.

- You must do the task in Writing Part 1.
- You read an email from a friend, a teacher or another person.
- You must write a reply to this email.
- The email has four notes on it. These notes help you with what you need to write.

- You must use all of the notes in your email.
- You need to write about 100 words.
- Part 1 carries the same number of marks as Part 2 of the writing paper.

Practice task

1 Read the task and write a first draft of your email. Write 100 words.

> Read this email from your English-speaking friend Jo and the notes you have made.

From: Jo
Subject: Weekend trip

Hi,

I'm really looking forward to our weekend trip to the city! — *Me too*
We must decide what to do and make a plan.

I'd quite like to go to the art gallery but you may not like that idea. Would you prefer to go there or to the museum? — *Say which you prefer*
We could also go to the theatre – there's a new musical on so we could see that in the evening. Would that be all right with you? — *No, because …*

Let me know if you have any suggestions for things to do! — *Tell Jo …*

See you soon,

Jo

How did you do?

2 Read the model email. Then compare it with your draft. Have you:
- responded to all the notes?
- used informal language?
- included an introduction and a conclusion?
- divided your email into paragraphs?
- started and ended your email in an appropriate way?
- checked your email for grammar and spelling mistakes?

From: Ewa
Subject: Weekend trip

Hi Jo,

Thanks for your email. I'm looking forward to our trip, too. ☐

It's a good idea to make a plan. I'd prefer to go to the museum, if that's OK with you. I'm not so interested in art and I think the museum has an interesting history exhibition. ☐

I haven't seen you for ages, so I'd rather spend the evening having a meal and talking. The theatre would be expensive and I don't want to spend lots of money. ☐

Could we go for a walk by the river on Sunday morning if the weather is fine? ☐

What do you think?

See you soon, ☐

Ewa

3 Complete the boxes in the email in Ex 2 with the correct numbers from the box.

> 1 Give reasons for your ideas.
> 2 Refer to your friend's email.
> 3 Use an appropriate phrase to end your email.
> 4 Make suggestions in a friendly way.
> 5 Use phrasal verbs and informal language.

Strategies and skills

Describing what you like, dislike, want and prefer

In an email, you often have to answer questions about what you like or don't like doing and what you want or prefer to do.

1 Put the expressions in the box into the correct columns in the table.

I dislike   I'd love to   I don't particularly like   I'd rather   I hate
I like … better   I love   I'm fond of   I'm keen on
I'm not very fond of   I'm particularly interested in
I prefer … to …   I really like   I think … is amusing   I want to
I wish   My favourite … is …   What I like least is …

What I like	What I don't like	What I want	What I prefer

2 Complete the sentences with the words in the box.

amusing   hate   is   love   not   of   really   than   to   would

1 I am very fond _____ going to concerts.
2 I prefer _____ go swimming when the weather's warm.
3 I'd rather stay in a hotel _____ go camping.
4 I _____ love to go hiking with you on Saturday.
5 I _____ enjoy watching nature documentaries on television – they're great.
6 I'm _____ particularly interested in art – it's boring.
7 I'd _____ to visit London one day.
8 My favourite sport _____ tennis.
9 I _____ cooking but I enjoy eating!
10 I think spending time with friends is _____ – we always have a good time.

Responding to an invitation

In an email you may have to respond politely to an invitation. You may accept it, reject it or suggest an alternative idea.

3 Look at each invitation. Does the person accept it (A), reject it (R) or suggest an alternative idea (S)?

1 A: Would you like to come to my house on Wednesday?
    B: Thanks for asking me but I'm afraid I'm busy then.
2 A: How about coming to the cinema with me tonight?
    B: That sounds good – I'd love to.
3 A: Shall we have coffee together tomorrow?
    B: I'm really busy tomorrow but how about Thursday?
4 A: Do you think you'd like to go shopping with me on Friday?
    B: That's a great idea – I can look for some new clothes.
5 A: It'd be great if you could come round tonight.
    B: Actually, I've got work to do so tomorrow would be better.
6 A: I'd like you to visit me next week if you can.
    B: Sounds good to me!
7 A: I'm having some friends round on Friday. Are you free?
    B: That's a pity – I've got cinema tickets for that night.

Making suggestions

4 Write suggestions about travelling to work using the prompts.

1 What about / catch / the bus / the office / ?
   _____
2 You should / get up earlier / so / can cycle / .
   _____
3 You could / share a car / a friend / .
   _____
4 You shouldn't / forget / check / the bus times / .
   _____
5 It's a good idea / work / home / some days / .
   _____

Giving reasons

TIP: In an email, it's polite to give a reason when you say what you like or prefer to do.

5 Match the things people like or prefer (1-7) with the reasons they give (A-G).

1 I really like skiing.
2 I'd rather go sightseeing on holiday.
3 I'm not keen on running.
4 I'm fond of cooking at home.
5 My favourite kind of music is pop.
6 I love spending time with friends.
7 I prefer studying history to maths.

A I like listening to different bands.
B I get tired after only going a few kilometres!
C It's lovely being in the mountains!
D I think it's more interesting.
E It's better than sitting on the beach all day.
F We often go shopping together in town.
G It's healthier than eating takeaways.

You can explain your reason using a linking word.

6 Choose the best word to complete the sentences.

1 I want to go to the cinema soon **and / otherwise** I'll miss that new film.
2 I enjoy playing football to keep fit, **although / so** I can't play very often.
3 I don't often eat fish **as / but** I don't like it much.
4 I wish I could learn to do yoga **because / but** people say it's quite difficult.
5 I like being outdoors in the countryside and **also / so** I often go hiking.

Including relevant information

7 Look at the task and the notes (1–4). The ideas (A–G) expand the notes but three of them are not relevant for the task. Match the ideas with the notes.

From: Sara
Subject: Birthday party

Hi,

It's Susie's birthday next week and I want to organise a party for her on Saturday afternoon. I've got some ideas and I'd like to know what you think.

We could have a barbecue in the garden or a picnic on the beach. What do you think she would prefer?

Have you got any ideas for a present I could buy her? I'm thinking of a book but I'm not sure.

I'd love some help with all this – can you do anything?

Thanks!

Jon

1 Give your opinion

2 Say which you prefer

3 Explain your idea …

4 Tell Jon …

A   Books are heavy to carry.
B   Great idea – she likes parties – lovely surprise.
C   I can't cook.
D   Picnic is better – less work to prepare – she loves being outside.
E   I love picnics.
F   I can tell all our friends about it.
G   She doesn't read books very often – how about a necklace?

8 A student has written an answer to the task but has missed out one of the notes. Expand the student's answer to include the missing information.

Hi Jon,

What a great idea! She loves parties and this would be a surprise for her.

I think that she would prefer a picnic. She loves being outside and it would be very easy for you to prepare – just sandwiches and cake.

I can contact all our friends on social media about when the party is. Would that help you?

See you soon!

Organising your answer

Your email should be organised clearly into paragraphs.

9 Look at the task below and the answer a student has written. They have written an answer but have not organised it into paragraphs. Rewrite the student's email, dividing it into paragraphs.

From: Andrea
Subject: Football tickets

Hi,

My football team's got an important game on Saturday at the local stadium and I'd love to go and watch.

I've had a look on the website and there are a few tickets available.

We could buy cheap seats right at the back or more expensive ones lower down. Which would you prefer?

I can pay for them now and you can give me the money later.

Best wishes,

Andrea

Agree

Respond

Say which you prefer

Thank Andrea

Hi Andrea,

Thanks for your email – that's great and I'd love to go, too! I'd always rather watch football live instead of on television and it's fantastic that we can still get tickets. I'd definitely prefer to be lower down though because I think there's no point in going if you can't see the game properly! So it's fine to get more expensive tickets. Thanks for offering to pay for them. As soon as you've bought them, let me know how much they cost and I'll send you the money. I'm looking forward to it! Best wishes, Abby

Using appropriate language

10 Correct the mistakes in these informal expressions from emails.

0 I'd love go with you.
I'd love **to** go with you.

1 Hi Agnes – great hear from you!

2 I was pleased getting your email this morning.

3 Please write me soon.

4 How about go to the cinema on Saturday?

5 Seeing you soon!

6 Best wish,

7 Let's meet at café in the High Street.

8 All best,

9 What you think?

10 That would great!

11 Thanks your email.

12 I was so happy to hearing your news!

11 Look again at the expressions in Ex 10. Put them into the correct column in the table.

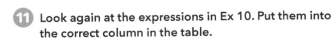

Beginning an email	Ending an email	In the middle of an email

EXAM TASK

Read this email from your English teacher Mr Lewis and the notes you have made.

> 👤 **From:** Mr Lewis
> **Subject:** College show
>
> I am looking for students to take part in a show at the end of the year. ●——— Great idea!
>
> I don't know whether to do a serious play or a musical. Which is better? ●——— Explain …
>
> I will need actors and singers, and people to help with the lighting. Could you let me know which you'd prefer? ●——— Tell Mr Lewis …
>
> I'd like to have a meeting for anyone interested next Monday evening. Is that a good time for you? ●——— No, because …

Write your **email** to Mr Lewis using **all the notes**.

- In Writing Part 2, you can choose to write an article.
- The article may be for an English-language magazine or a website.
- The aim of an article is to interest and engage the reader.
- You are told who you are writing the article for and given a title. There are also some questions for you to answer or ideas to include in your article.
- You need to write about 100 words.

Practice task

1 Read the task and write a first draft of your article. Write about 100 words.

> You see this announcement on an English-language website.

ARTICLES WANTED!

MY FAVOURITE SPORT

Tell us all about your favourite sport. When do you play or watch it? Why do you like it? Do you think it's important for everyone to play sport?

Write an article answering these questions and we will publish the best ones on our website.

Write your **article**.

How did you do?

2 Read the model article. Then compare it with your draft. Have you:

- answered all the questions?
- used interesting, informal language?
- included an introduction and a conclusion?
- divided your article into paragraphs?
- checked your article for grammar and spelling mistakes?

MY
FAVOURITE
SPORT

Do you love playing sport? ☐ I do! My favourite is field hockey, which I play at my local club. We practise twice a week and play matches on Sundays. We take part in a local league, so we play a different team every week.

I love it because it keeps me fit ☐, but more than that I enjoy being part of a team.

It's ☐ great to meet up with friends regularly and I love winning too, so I enjoy the competition!

I think it's important for everyone to play sport because it's healthy. It takes us out of our work or college routine. Everyone needs that! ☐

3 Complete the boxes in the example article in Ex 2 with the correct numbers from the box.

1. Begin your article with a question or a statement to interest the reader.
2. Finish in an interesting way.
3. Give your personal opinions, with reasons.
4. Use phrasal verbs, contractions and informal language.
5. Use the title given to you in the task.

Strategies and skills

Getting the right style

> **TIP:** Think about the kind of language you use so that your article has the right style.

1 If you speak directly to the reader using 'you' or 'we', it sounds friendly. Rewrite the sentences as questions so that they speak directly to the reader.

0 People often think that sport is expensive.

Do ___you think that sport is expensive___ ?

1 It is often said that people watch too much television.

Do _____ ?

2 Many people find sport interesting to watch.

Is _____ ?

3 A lot of people have never been to a live football match.

Have _____ ?

4 People think they are good at sport.

Do _____ ?

5 It's good when people are able to have a hobby they love.

Are _____ ?

6 People often find exercise difficult to do.

Do _____ ?

2 Rewrite the sentences using contractions where possible.

1 I have never thought about watching a live football match.

_____

2 It is very noisy when a goal is scored by the home team.

_____

3 I am going to learn to play tennis soon.

_____

4 There is an excellent leisure centre which is not too expensive.

_____

5 People will not do sport unless it is fun to do.

_____

6 I do not watch a lot of sport on television.

_____

3 You should use informal language to make your article seem friendly. Choose the informal option in each sentence.

1 It's **a great** / **a good** experience to be able to shout loud when my team scores.

2 **The use of** / **Using** technology can spoil the excitement of a game.

3 **I would say that** / **I think that** watching sport on TV with friends is fun.

4 It's **worthwhile** / **a good idea** to keep trying new things.

5 **I am afraid I cannot agree with that** / **I don't think that's right**.

6 **I'm really into sport** / **I take great pleasure in sport** of any kind.

Linking ideas

It is important to link your ideas clearly so that the reader can understand your article easily.

4 Match the sentence halves, then underline the word or phrase that links them.

1 Watching a film is good fun

2 As my brother is still at college

3 I want to work in tourism

4 Although it's raining,

5 It was such an interesting book

6 I'm quite good at football

7 My friend found the documentary so boring

8 I won't have time to meet you

A so that I can travel round the world.

B but my friend always beats me at tennis.

C and you can discuss it with friends afterwards.

D as I have to get home before 6 p.m.

E he has to study in the evenings.

F that he turned the TV off before the end.

G that I finished it in a day.

H I'll still go shopping.

5 Complete the second sentence so that it means the same as the first. Write one or two words.

1 He learnt French in order to get a job in France.

He learnt French _____ that he could get a job in France.

2 My sister knew I liked jazz so she bought me tickets to a jazz concert.

My sister bought me tickets to a jazz concert _____ she knew I liked jazz.

3 Although I don't usually like fish, that meal was delicious.

I don't usually like fish _____ that meal was delicious.

4 He travelled such a lot that he was never at home.

He travelled _____ much that he was never at home.

5 The work was boring, however, it was well paid.

I didn't enjoy the work _____ the pay was good.

Look at the exam task below. A student has written an article in answer to the task but is not sure how to link his ideas. For 1–7, choose the best alternative.

> You see this announcement in an English-language travel magazine.

ARTICLES WANTED!

MY PERFECT HOLIDAY

What would your perfect holiday be? Where would you go? Who would you go with? What would you do?

Write an article answering the questions and we will publish the best ones in our magazine.

Write your **article.**

My perfect holiday

I love holidays – who doesn't? I've already been on some wonderful trips ¹**but / such as** I still have lots of ideas about my perfect one.

I love hot weather ²**so / although** my perfect place would be sunny and warm. I would go to a beach ³**so that / so what** I could relax. ⁴**Because / So** I always enjoy being with my family, my perfect holiday would be with them. ⁵**As / So that** my sister loves sailing, I would like to do that with her. I ⁶**also / too** love playing tennis with my father ⁷**and / though** that would be important for this holiday.

I would love to go on this holiday – maybe I will next year!

Editing your work

> **TIP:** Always leave time in the exam to check and correct your written work.

7 **Look at the task below and the answer a student has written. They have forgotten to check their work and have made six mistakes with spelling and two with grammar. Correct the mistakes.**

> You see this announcement in an English-language shopping magazine.

ARTICLES WANTED! SHOPPING ADVICE

Do you enjoy shopping? Is there anything you enjoy buying? Why? What advice would you give someone about shopping in your town?

Write an article answering these questions and we will publish the most interesting in our magazine.

Write your **article.**

Shopping advice

Everyone loves shopping, don't they? Well, no, not me!

I can never to decide what to buy, espesially when I'm shopping for clothes. I hate going to crowded shops and waiting for ages in a queu to pay. I do enjoy buying presents, though, becuase I like giving other people something they realy like.

If anyone was shopping in my town, I'd say don't going at the weekend as the shops are really busy. Every Wendesday evening the shops are open late and they're quiter then.

Personally, though, I think shopping online is a much better idea!

> **TIP:** Always check your punctuation so that your meaning is clear for the reader.

 Add question marks and exclamation marks to the extract from an article below.

> Do you think it's important for people to spend their free time doing activities they enjoy, such as playing sport or listening to music. I think it is. If you don't have a hobby, then you can't enjoy life and I'd say that balancing work and free time is one of the most important things for us all to get right. I've managed to do this and it's great. I recommend you all do it, too.

Starting and ending an article

To catch the reader's attention, start by asking them a question about the topic that makes them think.

9 **Choose the best question, A or B, to start an article.**

1 Watching sport on TV
   A Do you really enjoy watching sport on TV?
   B Is there sport on TV where you live?

2 Travelling on holiday
   A Do you enjoy going on holiday?
   B We all go on holiday but what's the best way to travel?

3 The best place to live
   A I live in the countryside and I love it – but is it the best place for you?
   B Why do people enjoy living in cities?

4 The importance of museums
   A Is there a museum where you live?
   B I often go to museums but are they really important?

5 A good friend
   A How many friends should people have?
   B Have you got a really good friend?

Think about how to end your article in an interesting way. You can make a funny comment or a statement about the topic or you can summarise what you've been saying in your article.

10 Complete the sentences with the words in the box.

> clear   doubt   learn   needs   why   without

1 Everyone _____ a hobby in their life!
2 That's _____ I'll never give up hockey!
3 Therefore it's _____ that sport is important.
4 Life _____ holidays would be so boring!
5 Obviously we can _____ a lot by visiting museums!
6 There's no _____ that the city is the best place to live!

Giving personal opinions and reasons

When you give your personal opinion, try to add a reason if possible.

11 Complete the sentences with the words and phrases in the box.

> because   believe   can't understand   feel that
> for example   if   in my opinion   seems

1 You may not think I'm right but _____ learning another language is a useful hobby.
2 There are lots of reasons for taking up a new hobby, _____ meeting different people.
3 I think that festivals are important _____ they bring people together.
4 I _____ what the experts say about how important it is to eat healthy food.
5 It _____ to me that living in the countryside is both relaxing and enjoyable.
6 I _____ why anyone wouldn't like living in a city – there's so much to do!
7 It's difficult for people to learn to cook _____ they lead very busy lives and don't have much time.
8 I _____ my town is a great place to live. I love it and I'm going to stay here forever!

Including relevant information

TIP: You must answer all the questions you are asked in the task, but don't write too much because you might include irrelevant information.

12 Look at the task below and the answer a student has written. They have written too much and included information that is not necessary or is not relevant. Cross out the irrelevant sentences.

> You see this announcement in an English-language film magazine.

ARTICLES WANTED!

Films I like

What is your favourite kind of film? Why? Who do you like watching films with? Why? Are there any films you don't like?

Write an article answering these questions and we will print the best ones in the magazine.

Write your **article**.

Films I like

It's fun to go to watch a film, isn't it? But whether I enjoy it depends on the film. I love lots of different ones.

I started going to the cinema with my sister when I was about ten. My favourite kind of film is science fiction because I love the idea of being able to travel to other planets. I also enjoy the special effects that you can see in these films. I usually go to watch them with my friends, not my sister, because she prefers historical films.

There is a lovely cinema I like going to in my city and it has very big screens which are great for watching science-fiction films. I am not keen on musicals because I think they are not realistic and they are rather silly.

Watching a film is a great way of relaxing and that's why I like them!

EXAM TASK

You see this announcement on an English-language website.

ARTICLES WANTED!

THE TECHNOLOGY I USE

What technology do you use most — mobile phone, laptop or tablet? Why? Do you ever turn off your mobile phone? Would you like to spend less time using technology?

Write an article answering these questions and we will put the best ones on our website.

Write your **article**.

ABOUT THE TASK

- In Writing Part 2, you can choose to write a story.
- You are given the first sentence of the story. You must finish the story with your own ideas.
- You need to write about 100 words.

Practice task

1 Read the task and write a first draft of your story. Write about 100 words.

> Your English teacher has asked you to write a story.
> Your story must begin with this sentence.
> *When Sally heard the door of the changing room open, she turned around.*

Write your **story**.

How did you do?

2 Read the model story. Then compare it with your draft. Have you:

- followed on from the given first line?
- ordered the events logically using different tenses?
- used interesting and descriptive language?
- included an interesting ending?
- divided your story into paragraphs?
- checked your story for grammar and spelling mistakes?

3 Complete the boxes in the example story in Ex 2 with the correct numbers from the box.

> 1 Finish in an interesting or dramatic way.
> 2 Try to add some excitement to the story by asking questions or adding dialogue.
> 3 Try to use interesting language, such as verbs and adjectives.
> 4 Use different tenses to show the order of events.
> 5 Use time expressions to indicate when something happened.

When Sally heard the door of the changing room open, she turned around. She was surprised to see her friend Jo standing there looking very excited. Sally suddenly remembered that the football coach was announcing the team for their next important game but was she really good enough to have been chosen?

'You're in the team!' shouted Jo. Sally felt amazed and proud. She practised all week and when Saturday came she played better than she had ever played before. Just before the end of the game she even scored the winning goal.

Sally thought it had been the best day of her life so far!

Strategies and skills
Ordering events in a story
You can use different tenses to show when things happen.

> **TIP:** Before you start to write your story, think carefully about the order things will happen in. This will help you choose the correct tenses.

1 **Look at the paragraphs below. Number the events (A–D) in the order they happened.**

1 Jon ran into the cinema because he thought he was late. He sat down in his seat and opened the bag of sweets he had bought from a shop a few minutes earlier. The lights went out, the film started and he dropped the sweets all over the floor!

A Jon dropped the sweets.
B Jon bought some sweets.
C Jon opened the bag of sweets.
D The lights went out.

2 Susie heard a knock on the door. Her friend Sam had called her that morning to say she was coming to visit her but it was too early for her to arrive. Susie opened the door and laughed in surprise. The postman had put a huge parcel on the doorstep a few moments before knocking and it had her name on it.

A Susie opened the door.
B Susie heard a knock on the door.
C Sam called Susie.
D The postman put the parcel on the doorstep.

3 Alan felt in his coat pocket for his car keys. He knew he had put them there after he parked his car that morning but they weren't there now. Then he remembered. He had moved them into his bag when he left the office only a few moments ago!

A Alan put his car keys in his pocket.
B Alan moved his keys into his bag.
C Alan parked his car.
D Alan remembered where his keys were.

2 **Complete the sentences with the past simple or past perfect form of the verbs in brackets.**

1 She missed the bus because she _____ (got up) late that morning.

2 I got the job even though the interview last week _____ (not go) well.

3 She opened the present her friend had given her and _____ (feel) very happy.

4 When I woke up I realised it _____ (rain) a lot during the night.

5 He _____ (just / buy) his coffee when he realised he was also hungry so he bought a biscuit, too.

6 Her friend's flight _____ (arrive) late so she changed her plans for the day.

> **TIP:** You can also use time expressions to show when things happen.

3 **Choose the best time expressions to complete the story.**

Cooking for friends

I had invited some friends to dinner but I'm not a very good cook. I decided to make pasta because I thought it was easy. **¹In the beginning / First of all** I put water in the pan and then I turned on the cooker. **²Just as / During** I was checking the other ingredients there was a knock at the door. **³Then / When** I went to answer it, it was my neighbour and we chatted for a few minutes. **⁴Suddenly / At once** I smelled something bad! I **⁵at the time / immediately** ran to the kitchen to see what it was. I hadn't put enough water in the pan and **⁶now / before** it was dry. The metal pan was very hot and the smell was terrible. Luckily, **⁷as soon as / later** I opened all the windows the smell began to disappear. However, **⁸the moment / finally** my friends arrived I told them I wanted to order a pizza!

4 Complete the sentences with time expressions from the box.

> as soon as   before   earlier   first   immediately   when

1 I wasn't having a good time so I left _____ I could.
2 I had a lot of things to remember so _____ I made a list so I didn't forget anything, then I went to the shop.
3 It's never a good idea to leave _____ the end of a sports match – you might miss a goal!
4 I was sleeping _____ I heard the window break so I jumped out of bed and ran downstairs.
5 The concert was great so I was glad I had bought a ticket a few weeks _____ .
6 When the phone rang I picked it up _____ because I knew it was important.

Using descriptive language

> **TIP:** Use a variety of language to make your story more interesting and try not to repeat the same words often.

You can make a story more interesting if you add adjectives and don't repeat words.

5 Look at the story below. It isn't very interesting to read because of the language used. Replace the underlined words with the more interesting words in the box.

> determined   encouraged   exhausted
> reached   spectators   shouting

The race was nearly over. Ahmed was tired but he was ¹<u>keen</u> to win. There were only three people in front of him and he knew he could go faster. He could hear the ²<u>people watching</u> ³<u>saying</u> his name and this ⁴<u>helped</u> him to try harder. He ran faster and then he passed two of the people. Now there was only one person ahead of him. He felt ⁵<u>tired</u> but he ⁶<u>got to</u> the finish line first.

6 Replace 'nice' in the paragraph below with the adjectives in the box.

> comfortable   delicious   enjoyable   exciting
> friendly   fun   large   sandy

Staying in the holiday resort was ¹nice because there were lots of ²nice activities to do, like rock climbing. The beach was ³nice. The rooms in the hotel were ⁴nice – we had a lot of space and the beds were ⁵nice. The food in the restaurant was ⁶nice, too, and all the waiters were very ⁷nice. In fact, it was a very ⁸nice trip!

> **TIP:** You can add interest by giving more details.

7 Compare the pairs of paragraphs below. Which one is more interesting? Answer the questions.

A **i)** Abbi had lost touch with a girl she was very friendly with at college. She was quite upset about this so she tried very hard to find her using social media. After a long search she managed to get her address and finally made contact. They met and had a great time!

ii) Abbi didn't know what happened to a girl she knew at college. She wanted to know what happened to her so she used social media. She got her address and called her. They met.

1 How close was Abbi to the girl at college?
2 How did Abbi feel when they lost touch?
3 Did Abbi find her friend quickly?
4 Did they have a good time when they met?

B **i)** The rain was so heavy that the two friends got really wet as soon as they left the station. Marc had forgotten to take his raincoat so he was feeling very uncomfortable. His friend had a jacket so he was feeling a little better! By the time they had walked all the way home, Marc was very miserable.

ii) It was raining so the friends got wet when they left the station. Marc didn't have his raincoat, which was bad. His friend was wearing a jacket. They walked all the way home.

5 How bad was the rain?
6 How quickly did they get wet?
7 Why did Marc get so wet?
8 How did Marc feel when he got home?

Planning a story

> **TIP:** If you plan your story with a beginning, a middle and an end, it will be easier to write.

8 **Look at the first line of a story. Answer the questions.**

I was on holiday with friends when I decided to go cycling in the mountains.

1 Beginning: What happened first?
  How did I feel? Why?
2 Middle: What problem did I have?
  How did I feel about it?
3 End: What happened at the end?

9 **Look at a student's story. How did she answer the questions in Ex 8 in her story?**

I was on holiday with friends when I decided to go cycling in the mountains. It was wonderful to be in the fresh air. The sky was blue, the air was warm and I felt happy.

After three hours I was hungry, so I stopped at a small café for lunch. I ate some sandwiches, which were delicious. When I went to pay, I realised I had left my money in the hotel. I felt embarrassed. Fortunately, a girl who was having coffee with her sister offered to pay. I felt very grateful.

We still message each other so I found a new friend that day!

Ending your story

Think about your ending before you start writing so that it has more dramatic effect.

10 **Look at the first sentence of a story. The story includes getting lost and feeling scared. Look at the three endings (A–C) below. Which one do you think is the most interesting?**

On the last day of the holiday, I decided to go exploring on my own in the forest.

A I used my mobile phone to call my friends who came to find me. Once they arrived we all went back to the hotel. Then we had dinner together in the restaurant, which was very nice.

B I walked back to the hotel and told my friends all about getting lost in the forest. They were surprised and told me not to do it again!

C I wandered around for what felt like hours. Suddenly I felt something touch my leg and I realised it was a small white dog. It ran in front of me and led me to the hotel. My friends rushed out and asked 'Where have you been?' I felt happy to see them but I had no idea where the dog came from.

Adding a title

Although you don't have to write a title, if you think of one, it can help you write an interesting story.

11 **Look at the story plans below and choose the most interesting title for each one.**

1 A family go to beach for the day – weather is bad – they have to stay in a hotel – go home early
  A A rainy day
  B The worst day out
2 A boy hears a strange noise – goes to look out of the window – sees a man stealing his bike – calls the police – gets bike back
  A Lost bike
  B Some good luck
3 A girl goes shopping – finds a wallet – finds owner who is famous singer – gives her a ticket to a concert
  A An unexpected event
  B A good concert

> **EXAM TASK**
>
> **Write your answer in about 100 words.**
>
> Your English teacher has asked you to write a story.
>
> Your story must begin with this sentence.
>
> *As soon as Mario woke up, he realised something was different.*
>
> Write your **story**.

ABOUT THE TASK

- In Listening Part 1, you hear seven unrelated short extracts. These can be dialogues such as conversations or monologues such as announcements, voicemail messages, broadcasts and so on.
- There is one question about each extract.
- There are three pictures (A, B and C) under each question. You listen and choose the picture that answers the question.

- The questions ask about practical things from daily life and the pictures may include prices, times, gifts, activities and so on.
- In the recording, things in all three pictures will be mentioned but only one answers the question.
- You have time to read the questions and look at the pictures before you listen. You hear each extract twice.
- There is one mark for each correct answer.

Practice task

1 🎧 L01 Listen to four extracts. For each question, choose the correct answer.

1 Which sound does the woman prefer?

2 What does the man decide to do with his friends?

3 What will the woman buy for her sister's wedding?

4 What time does the show start?

How did you do?

2 Check your answers.

3 Look at the audioscript for Ex 1 question 1. Are the following statements true or false?

A The woman likes birds less than other sounds.

B The woman finds the sound of waves relaxing.

C The woman is happy when she hears a baby laugh.

M: That programme about how different sounds make people feel was interesting.

F: Yes, it made me think! I like lots of different things. The sound of waves on a beach is relaxing – I feel quite calm when I hear that. But when my sister had a baby I loved hearing him laugh – I felt so happy. They mentioned birds singing in the programme and that can be lovely, though not my personal favourite. I always like anything connected with my family best!

4 Underline the sentences in the audioscript in Ex 3 that tells you that she likes the sound of a baby best.

5 Look at the audioscript for Ex 1 question 2 and answer the questions.

1 The answer to question 2 in Ex 1 is C. Why doesn't he want to go shopping?
   A There are too many people in town.
   B His friends don't want to go.

2 Why doesn't he want to play a computer game?
   A The weather is too good to stay indoors.
   B He's bored because it's what he usually does.

F: What are you going to do with your friends this afternoon?

M: I'm not sure – they've left the decision to me. I know that some of them want to go shopping, but the town will be so busy. The weather looks nice, so I guess going out for a cycle ride is the best plan – and we haven't done that for ages, so it'll be fun. It isn't great sitting inside playing computer games when the weather's good, even though that's usually my choice.

6 Underline the sentence in the audioscript in Ex 5 that tells you that he wants to go cycling.

7 Look at the audioscript for Ex 1 question 3 and answer the questions.

1 The answer to the question is B. Why doesn't she buy a kettle?
   A Her brother has already bought one.
   B She thinks it's too modern.

2 What is the problem with the vase?
   A Her grandmother has already bought one.
   B She doesn't find it exciting.

F: My sister's getting married soon and I want to buy her something nice.

M: Have you got any ideas?

F: I thought about some mugs, but she's already got lots of those. My brother's buying them a really nice kettle – it's very modern! I wish I'd thought of that. I could get a pretty vase, but it's not very exciting, and my grandmother is probably getting that. I think I'll go with my first idea – after all, you can never have too many of them!

M: It's your choice.

8 Underline the sentences in the audioscript in Ex 7 that tell you that she is going to buy the mugs.

9 Look at the audioscript for Ex 1 question 4. The answer to the question is C. Underline the parts of the audioscript that answer the questions.

1 What is happening at 6.30?
2 What is happening at 7?
3 How do you know that the show starts at 7.30?

Hi, Clarrie – just to let you know that I'm going to be late tonight – I wanted to leave the office at 5 but something's come up and I can't leave until 6. There's a café opposite the theatre that's open until 6:30, so you can get something to eat before the show. If I'm not there by 7, don't wait for me, I'll meet you inside the theatre. I'll have plenty of time to get there before the curtain goes up at 7:30 so I won't miss anything.

Strategies and skills
Predicting what you will hear

> **TIP:** Listen for information about the options that will help you choose the right answer.

It is easier to get the right answer if you can predict what to listen for.

1 Look at the questions and sets of pictures below. What kind of words do you think you need to listen for? Tick all the words that will help you work out the answer to the question.

1 Which jacket did the man buy?

> buttons   jacket   one   pocket   size   two

2 How much did the woman pay for the theatre tickets?

> cheap   choice   easy   expensive   view   website

3 Which sport is the man's favourite?

> ball   best   goal   individual   prefer

2 🎧 **L02** Listen to the extracts and choose the correct answers in Ex 1. Did you hear the words you ticked? Why did they help you?

Words like *but* and *although* can help you to work out the correct answer.

3 Look at the words in bold in the sentence beginnings. Choose the best ending (A or B) for each sentence.

1 I love watching football **though**
  A most of my friends don't.
  B it's on television in the evenings.

2 I hate going to the supermarket **but**
  A it's always so busy.
  B I need to buy some food.

3 My family are thinking of moving to the countryside **although**
  A I'm not particularly keen on the idea.
  B it's a fantastic idea.

4 The film wasn't very good **so**
  A I left before the end.
  B I enjoy historical dramas.

5 **Because** it's my grandparents' wedding anniversary
  A I didn't send them a card.
  B I'll visit them tonight.

6 I'm working late in the office tonight **as**
  A I have such a lot to finish.
  B it's situated in the city.

7 I'm meeting my friend for coffee, **and then**
  A I'll do some shopping.
  B I haven't seen her for ages.

8 I must go to the gym tonight **even though**
  A it's good for me.
  B I find it boring.

9 I do a lot of sport – **in fact**
  A I'm training to run a marathon.
  B the equipment is expensive.

10 I have a busy morning routine, **including**
  A before I go to work.
  B making breakfast for the family.

4 🎧 **L03 Listen to the extracts. For each question, choose the correct answer.**

1 Which book is the man's favourite?

2 What did the woman do on her birthday?

Discuss or answer.

1 What are the advantages and disadvantages of living with other people?

2 Think of a time you made a complaint about something. What happened?

Listening for specific information

TIP: The people in the extracts in the task will mention every option, but only one is the answer.

5 **Look at the sentences below and answer the questions.**

1 I thought about buying a bowl but it was very expensive and small. I did like it, though.
  A Did she buy the bowl?
  B How do you know?

2 I wanted to go swimming today, even though it was cold, but I changed my mind. I'll go next week.
  A Did he go swimming today?
  B How do you know?

3 I didn't enjoy my holiday because although the food was great, the weather wasn't.
  A What spoiled her holiday?
  B How do you know?

4 I love music and I listen to it a lot, but I'm not as keen on it as playing computer games.
  A What does he like best?
  B How do you know?

5 I wanted to get her a nice birthday present and I looked at some perfume and then some gloves. In the end I couldn't find any of those to fit her, so I went back to my first idea.
  A What present did she buy?
  B How do you know?

6 I'm doing a photography course and we had to take photos of interesting buildings. I looked everywhere and found an old house, but in the end I went for a modern glass one.
  A What did he photograph?
  B How do you know?

7 I'm going to meet Peter at 5 p.m. at the latest.
  A Could she meet Peter before 5 p.m.?
  B How do you know?

8 My friend asked to watch television so I agreed to do that, too, though I really wanted to go out.
  A Did she decide to go out?
  B How do you know?

6 **Choose the word or phrase in each set that has a different meaning to the others.**

1 prefer   rather   like more   take part

2 the best   OK   top of my list   favourite

3 choose   go for   do   decide on

4 like   hate   keen on   fond of

5 on my way   during the journey   nearby   while travelling

6 where   there   at that place   next to the bank

7 **Complete the sentences using a word or phrase from Ex 6.**

1 I went to a wonderful concert last night and I'll never forget it. I've been to many concerts but this was _____ performance I've ever seen.

2 Jo will be in the café at 7 p.m. so I can meet her _____ .

3 Don't forget we need some bread and milk – if you don't have time, then I can go to the supermarket _____ home. Let me know!

4 I have always enjoyed history and I think the seventeenth century is my _____ period.

5 I watch television quite a lot but I'm not _____ those dramas – they can be rather dark.

6 I definitely _____ orange juice to apple juice – I drink quite a lot of it!

7 It's difficult to _____ what to eat – everything looks so good!

8 I've made my final choice – I'm going to _____ the fish!

Understanding distraction

> **TIP:** If you're not sure of the answer, think about why the other options are not correct.

8 🎧 **L04 Look at the questions below. You have been given the answer and the audioscript. Listen and read, and decide why the other options are wrong.**

1 What does the man want to eat at the restaurant? (Answer: A)

F: What do you want to eat? I'm going for the pizza.

M: I'm not sure. I had fish last week so I don't want that again. I know the pies are good here so that's a possibility. I often have Italian food so a change would be nice.

F: You'll have to decide soon!

M: It's difficult – but OK – I'll have the same as you.

2 Which souvenir did the woman buy on holiday? (Answer: B)

M: Did you bring anything back from your holiday?

F: I wanted a souvenir but it wasn't easy to decide what to get. Some of the things, like a ceramic plate I saw, were just too expensive. The T-shirts were reasonable so I went for one of those. What I would have loved, though, was this beautiful painting. I didn't have any space in my suitcase for it, which was a pity!

3 What date is the wedding? (Answer: C)

M: When is your sister getting married?

F: Well, it was originally planned for the 6th of May, but then some of our cousins couldn't come over from America at that time. So she moved it to the 15th of May, which suited everybody. There was some talk of it happening on the 12th of May instead, because it was better for some of her friends, but she didn't change her plans.

4 What course is the man going to do? (Answer: C)

F: What are you going to study at college?

M: Well, I planned to do IT but I don't have the right qualifications, so that's out. My parents hoped I'd do something in finance because they thought that could lead to a good job, but I wasn't really very keen. I wanted to study something I really enjoyed so I'm going to do photography. It should be better than the other options!

🎧 **L05 For each question, choose the correct answer.**

1 How will the family travel to the coast?

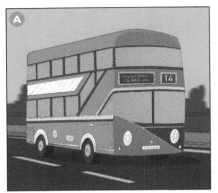  

2 What does the woman decide to do at the weekend?

3 What will the weather be like tomorrow?

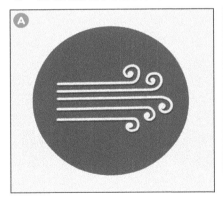  

4 What did the woman see on her holiday?

5 Where will the man go first?

6 How much was the woman's winter coat?

7 Which musical instrument does the man enjoy playing most?

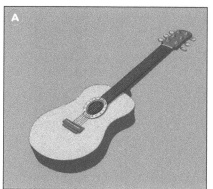
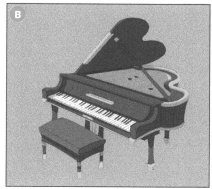
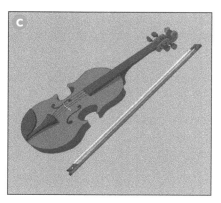

ABOUT THE TASK

- In Listening Part 2, you hear six different extracts. They are all short conversations between two people.
- The context sentence says who is speaking and about what.
- There is one question about each extract with three multiple-choice options (A, B and C). You choose the option that answers the question.

- You may be asked about one speaker's feelings, attitude or opinions, or whether the two speakers agree with each other.
- You have time to read the questions and options before you listen and you hear each extract twice.
- There is one mark for each correct answer.

Practice task

1 🎧 **L06 Listen to three extracts. For each question, choose the correct answer.**

1 You will hear a man telling a friend about his new job. How does he feel about it?
   A nervous about meeting new colleagues
   B unhappy about the hours he has to work
   C worried about being able to do it well

2 You will hear a woman telling a friend about an advertisement she has seen on television. What does she think about it?
   A It gives useful information.
   B It uses annoying music.
   C It has interesting images.

3 You will hear two friends talking about a photography exhibition they went to. They agree that
   A the gallery was impressive.
   B the photographs were interesting.
   C the cost of the entry ticket was reasonable.

How did you do?

2 Check your answers.

3 Question 1 in Ex 1 tests your understanding of the man's feelings. Look at the highlighted words.

1 What does 'happy' relate to? **working hours / people / job**
2 What does 'relaxed' relate to? **working hours / people / job**
3 What does 'stressed' relate to? **working hours / people / job**

Woman:	Are you enjoying your new job?
Man:	Well, yes and no. I'm definitely happy about the people I work with – they're very kind and help me if I'm not sure what to do. It's a much better working situation, too. They told me at the interview I don't have to be in the office at a particular time every day, which makes me feel relaxed. It means the travelling is easier – the buses aren't reliable and in my old job I was often late. The only thing I get stressed about is whether I'm good enough, which is a bit difficult to deal with.

4 Question 2 in Ex 1 tests your understanding of the woman's opinion. Look at the highlighted sentences and answer the questions.

1 Does she say that the information is useful or the advert doesn't give enough information?
2 Does she like the music, or find it annoying?
3 Does she say that the images are interesting? What word does she use for this?

Woman:	That advertisement always seems to be on television.
Man:	You mean the one for breakfast cereal?
Woman:	Yes, I've seen it a lot, and the soundtrack's terrific – it's difficult to forget! I often sing it even though I don't buy the cereal.
Man:	I buy it and it's quite tasty.
Woman:	Well, I don't really know enough about it – the advert doesn't say how much sugar there is in it. So that's not good – even if the graphics are actually rather cool! It's one of the better adverts in that respect.

5 Question 3 in Ex 1 tests your understanding of whether the speakers agree or not. Match the highlighted sentences with the options in Question 3 and answer the questions below.

1 Who thinks the gallery was impressive?
2 Who thinks the photographs were interesting?
3 Who thinks the cost of the entry ticket was reasonable?

Man:	I loved that exhibition!
Woman:	Yes, I thought it was spectacular. ¹The place where the photographs were displayed was incredible.
Man:	²I found that sometimes the lighting made them difficult to see – but ³the subjects were fascinating. I love seeing plants and animals in their natural surroundings. It helps me look at them in a new way.
Woman:	⁴I spent ages looking at them because there was so much to see. That was great, though ⁵I did feel a bit annoyed about how much it was to go in.
Man:	⁶It must be expensive to put on an exhibition like that so I didn't mind that. I might even go again.

Strategies and skills

Identifying a speaker's attitude

> **TIP:** If a question asks 'What does the speaker think?' then you need to listen for their attitude or opinion.

1 A speaker shows their attitude and opinion about something by the words they choose to use. Look at what the speakers say. What is their opinion?

1 I don't know what to do – it's incredibly hard to make a decision.
   A The decision is very difficult to make.
   B The decision is impossible to make.

2 Do you really think it's a good idea to go in January? It will be very cold.
   A I think we should go in January.
   B I'm not sure that we should go in January.

3 Thank you for your advice but I'm going to make up my own mind.
   A I don't agree with your advice so I shall decide myself.
   B I'm happy that you gave me some advice and it was useful.

4 That TV documentary was a waste of my time.
   A I didn't enjoy the documentary but it passed the time.
   B I wish I had done something else instead of watching the documentary.

5 It's not nice if you win a sports competition and then have to give an interview.
   A Giving an interview spoils the fun of winning a competition.
   B Giving an interview adds to the pleasure of winning a competition.

6 People expect too much of celebrities – they're only human!
   A Celebrities are often misunderstood.
   B Celebrities are lucky to live the way they do.

2 Read the pairs of sentences below. Are the speakers saying the same thing (S), or something different (D)?

1 A: I'm afraid there's too much sport on television.
   B: I wish they would show less sport on television.

2 A: Everyone must have a holiday every year.
   B: It's necessary to take a break from work once a year.

3 A: Science fiction is always unrealistic, and I'm not that keen on it.
   B: We can learn a lot from science fiction, and it makes me curious to find out more.

4 A: No one needs to read newspapers now because everyone looks at social media instead.
   B: Some people can't get the internet, and my grandfather buys a newspaper every day.

5 A: Listening to music is a great way to help me concentrate on my studies.
   B: It find it very hard to study if there's no noise so having music in the background is useful.

6 A: Bad weather makes me feel miserable, wherever I am.
   B: I love listening to the wind and rain outside and it's even exciting being outside in it!

7 A: The concert was wonderful, and the orchestra played beautifully.
   B: I've heard better orchestras and so I left the concert early.

8 A: People should try to avoid social media one day every week, otherwise it can be addictive and stressful.
   B: Using social media every day can be bad for you.

3 🎧 **L07 Listen to six speakers. For each question, choose the best answer.**

1 What does the man think about his holiday?
  A It was really good fun.
  B It was rather disappointing.

2 What does the woman think about the film?
  A The music was pleasant.
  B The acting was very good.

3 What does the man think about his birthday party?
  A It was such a surprise that he couldn't enjoy it very much.
  B He regretted that it took place after work.

4 What does the woman think about her college course?
  A The lectures are all extremely interesting.
  B The timetable is not very convenient.

5 What does the man think about buying expensive clothes?
  A It can be a good idea.
  B It sometimes wastes money.

6 What does the woman think about her new job?
  A There are many disadvantages.
  B It is rather confusing at times.

SPEAKING BOOST

Discuss or answer.

1 When was the last time you were interviewed for a job or other opportunity? What happened?

2 How would a close friend describe you?

Listening for agreement or disagreement

TIP: If you are asked whether the speakers agree, you won't hear them say 'I agree' or 'I don't agree'. You need to think about what they are saying and decide whether they are saying the same thing.

4 **Match the statements (1–8) and the responses (A–H). Do the phrases in bold indicate that the speakers agree or disagree?**

1 I think it's important for people to think about the mistakes they make.
2 It's important to have friends.
3 I hate paying a lot in a restaurant.
4 It's vital to share the same interests with friends.
5 Not many people read books nowadays.
6 Holidays are unnecessary and expensive.
7 I love science-fiction films!
8 I think that football is boring.

A **Certainly** some food can be overpriced.
B **Are you sure** about that? Everyone needs a break!
C **I'm not sure** that's true – I read a lot.
D **In my opinion** you just don't understand it!
E **Well**, my friends like very different things from me.
F **That's true, but** not too many otherwise they're not real.
G **Unfortunately**, that's not how I feel about them.
H **That's certainly** a good way for people to learn.

5 🎧 **L08 Listen to the short conversations. Do the speakers agree with each other or not?**

1 You will hear two friends talking about failure.
  Do they agree or disagree about it?

2 You will hear two people talking about how people learn.
  Do they agree or disagree about it?

3 You will hear two friends talking about making a first impression.
  Do they agree or disagree about it?

4 You will hear two people talking about job interviews.
  Do they agree or disagree about them?

5 You will hear two people talking about meeting someone for the first time.
  Do they agree or disagree about it?

6 You will hear two friends talking about body language.
  Do they agree or disagree about it?

7 You will hear two people talking about having friends.
  Do they agree or disagree about it?

8 You will hear two friends talking about a film.
  Do they agree or disagree about it?

Identifying a speaker's feelings

TIP: People often use different words to describe their feelings. You may not hear the same word as you see in the option although the meaning may be similar.

6 Look at the words and phrases describing feelings below. Choose the word or phrase in each set that has a different meaning to the others.

1	**A** jealous	**B** want the same	**C** embarrassed
2	**A** frightened	**B** afraid	**C** disappointed
3	**A** annoyed	**B** anxious	**C** angry
4	**A** surprised	**B** pleased	**C** glad
5	**A** worried	**B** nervous	**C** sorry
6	**A** sure	**B** confused	**C** certain
7	**A** depressed	**B** bored	**C** sad
8	**A** interested	**B** fascinated	**C** excited
9	**A** hopeful	**B** relieved	**C** want something to happen
10	**A** enthusiastic	**B** tired	**C** exhausted

7 Read what eight speakers say. Choose the correct option to describe how each person feels.

1 The boss can't expect me to work extra hours this week – I have things to do!
A surprised about having to work extra hours
B annoyed about being asked to work extra hours

2 I'm really looking forward to the trip on Saturday – I can't wait!
A excited about going on the trip
B sure that the trip will be successful

3 I don't know what I have to do – I wish I understood it better.
A interested in what to do
B confused about what to do

4 It's a good thing we've bought our tickets – the concert is sold out now.
A angry that there are no more tickets
B relieved that they have already bought tickets

5 My new job looks quite hard and I don't know whether I can do it.
A frightened about starting a new job
B positive that they will be able to do the job

6 What a pity it's raining – I really wanted to play tennis today.
A disappointed about the weather
B glad that they can't play tennis

7 It's incredible how difficult it can be to learn another language.
A surprised about how difficult it is
B pleased about being able to learn it

8 I really admire my sister – she's a wonderful musician!
A jealous of their sister
B impressed by their sister

Understanding functions/purpose

TIP: Questions may ask you what someone is doing when they speak, or why they are speaking.

When we speak we use different functions such as giving advice.

8 Look at the sentences below and choose the best option.

1 It's much better for you to go by bus because parking is difficult in town.

What is the speaker doing?
A giving advice
B describing a situation

2 Can we meet at 7 instead of 6? I have to work late tonight.

Why is the speaker calling?
A to ask for a favour
B to offer to change an arrangement

3 That was a really bad meal – I didn't enjoy it at all!

What is the speaker doing?
A complaining about the meal
B explaining something that was wrong

4 I think it's probably a good idea to check the route before we set off.

What is the speaker doing?
A making a suggestion
B offering to make a decision

5 The first part of the film is in the city and it's really exciting. You should see it!

What is the speaker doing?
A describing the film
B recommending the film

6 I'm sure you'll win the race even though you're a bit nervous now.

What is the speaker doing?
A warning the runner about the race
B encouraging the runner

🎧 **L09** **For each question, choose the correct answer.**

1   You will hear two friends talking about a film they have just seen.

They both think that
A   the story wasn't clear.
B   the acting wasn't good.
C   the locations weren't interesting.

2   You will hear a woman telling a friend about a bus journey she made.

What is she doing?
A   complaining about how long the bus took
B   describing the route the bus took
C   explaining why she took the bus

3   You will hear a man telling a friend about his holiday.

What did he enjoy most about it?
A   the activities he was able to do
B   the location of the hotel
C   the people he met there

4   You will hear two friends talking about buying music.

What does the woman dislike about buying music online?
A   how much it usually costs
B   how long it can take
C   how difficult it is to buy individual songs

5   You will hear two friends talking about a new computer game.

  What do they agree about it?
  A It is relaxing to play.
  B It takes up a lot of time.
  C It is better than other activities.

6   You will hear a woman telling a friend about a coat she has just bought.

  How does she feel about it?
  A disappointed with the colour
  B unhappy about the price she paid
  C unsure whether she made the right choice

TEST

- In Listening Part 3, you hear one long recording. Only one person is speaking. This person may be making a presentation, giving a talk or making an announcement.

- There's a context sentence that tells you who's speaking and what they're talking about.

- There are six notes or sentences about the recording, with one gap in each. The sentences or notes are not linked together.

- You listen and fill in the gaps with one or two words, a number, a date or a time.

- You write exactly what you hear in each gap. You mustn't change the word you hear in any way and you must spell the word correctly.

- You have time to read the task before you listen and you hear the recording twice.

- There is one mark for each correct answer.

Practice task

> **TIP:** Make sure that you spell the word you write in the gap correctly.

1 🎧 **L10 For each question, write the correct answer in the gap. Write one or two words or a number or a date or a time.**

You will hear a woman called Selina giving a presentation about learning to make pots in her art class.

Selina decided to make pots after seeing a large **(1)** _____ of them.

Selina says the pots feel **(2)** _____ and wet to touch when she's making them.

Selina likes painting **(3)** _____ on her pots to make them beautiful.

Selina thinks she will sell her pots for **(4)** £_____ each.

How did you do?

2 **Check your answers.**

3 **Look at the audioscript for Ex 1 question 1. Answer the questions.**

1 How many different courses are mentioned?
2 Why did Selina decide to make pots?

Hi, I'm Selina and I want to tell you about my pottery class. I'm quite a creative person and I've always enjoyed making things with my hands. One day I saw a large poster showing different courses available at the college. One of them was making furniture, but it didn't look very interesting. Another was making toys, which looked like fun. I wasn't totally sure, though, until I went to a big exhibition of pots and decided that's what I wanted to make.

4 **Look at the audioscript for Ex 1 question 2. Answer the questions.**

1 What does Selina touch?
2 Which two words does she use to describe how it feels? What do you notice about these two words in question 2?

Now I'm learning to make pots with my hands. I work with something called clay, which is amazing to touch – to me it feels wet and soft. I put this clay on a round plate that turns around very fast and as it's turning I make it into whatever shape I want my pot to be. It's very difficult and sometimes it all goes wrong!

5 **Look at the audioscript for Ex 1 question 3. Answer the questions.**

1 What did Selina paint on her pots in the past?
2 What does Selina paint on her pots now?

Once I've finished making a pot I put it into a hot oven and bake it until it's hard. After that I take it out and leave it to cool. That's when I can paint it. I used to like painting flowers on my pots but these days I prefer birds. They're very beautiful!

6 **Look at the audioscript for Ex 1 question 4. Answer the questions.**

1 How many numbers do you hear?
2 Which one answers the question?

I usually give my pots as gifts to friends but I'd like to be able to sell them in the future. I don't expect to make hundreds of pounds – one student on the course has sold a pot for £35, though I'd be happy to take £20 at the moment!

7 🎧 **L11 Listen to the whole recording again and check your answers.**

Strategies and skills

Listening for figures

> **TIP:** Write numbers as numerals rather than words where you can.

In the exam task you may need to write numbers in your answer. These may be dates, times, prices or numbers.

1 🎧 **L12 Listen and tick the number or date you hear.**

1	A	4th November	B	14th November
2	A	1990	B	1999
3	A	6:50	B	6:15
4	A	7:20	B	7:12
5	A	£5.95	B	£5.05
6	A	230	B	2030

2 🎧 **L13 Listen to the recording and write the correct number in the gap.**

1 Chloe's birthday is on _____ .

2 Gemma was born in _____ .

3 Sara thinks the train leaves at _____ .

4 Adam thinks the film begins at _____ .

5 Jac says she paid £_____ for the book.

6 Luke expects _____ people to come to the conference.

SPEAKING BOOST

Discuss or answer.

1 If you could learn a new skill, what would you choose? Why?

2 Describe the best exhibition or live event you have been to.

Listening for spelling

> **TIP:** If you are asked to spell a word, you need to write it correctly.

Some words can sound very similar but are spelled differently.

3 🎧 **L14 Listen and choose the word you hear the speaker spell.**

1	A	where	B	wear
2	A	weather	B	whether
3	A	their	B	there
4	A	back	B	bag
5	A	arrive	B	alive
6	A	sit	B	seat

4 🎧 **L15 The student has made one mistake with spelling in each sentence below. Listen and correct it.**

1 The website address is www.delardang.com.

2 Please email Ganicewethur@history.com.

3 The school is called Laykort Academy.

4 The address you want is 24, Alwormter Street.

5 You should contact Peter Hisdorcutt.

6 The town is in the north and it's called Pirchering.

Identifying the kind of information you need

> **TIP:** Read the text before you listen and think about what kind of word you need to write in each gap. It could be a number, a place, a time, an activity, etc.

If you know the kind of word you need to listen for, it is easier to identify the answer when you listen.

5 **Look at eight sentences from different tasks. Choose the kind of word you need to complete each one.**

1 Ali says that the _____ was what she enjoyed most about her last holiday. **person / activity**

2 Robbie decided to go to Paris after a _____ suggested it. **person / thing**

3 Sally thinks _____ is early enough in the evening to meet. **time / date**

4 Sami is pleased that he only paid £_____ for his coat. **number / price**

5 Fabia bought a(n) _____ as a gift. **price / object**

6 In the science museum the _____ was the most popular with visitors. **person / object**

7 The tour starts at the _____ . **time / place**

8 There were a total of _____ people in the race. **number / person**

6 🎧 **L16 Listen and complete the sentences in Ex 5.**

Identifying incorrect answers

> **TIP:** Listen carefully to all the possible answers before you choose what to write. You can confirm your answer the second time you listen.

You will hear more than one answer that you think might be possible but only one will be correct.

7 🎧 **L17 Look at the short task and listen to the recording. Complete the sentences.**

EDA'S MODEL CAR COLLECTION

Eda began collecting model cars when her **(1)** _____ gave her one as a present.

Eda now owns more than **(2)** _____ model cars.

Eda enjoys looking for model cars in **(3)** _____ .

Eda paid **(4)** £_____ for a car she is very pleased with.

8 Look at the audioscript for Ex 7 and answer the questions.

1 Why is 'father' wrong for question 1?
   A He didn't give Eda a car.
   B He didn't collect model cars.

2 Why is '100' wrong for question 2?
   A The question asks about 'now' and that was in the past.
   B Eda doesn't say 'over' 100.

3 Why is 'sales' wrong for question 3?
   A Eda doesn't buy cars in sales.
   B Eda says she finds sales 'stressful', not enjoyable.

4 Why is '150' wrong for question 4?
   A It's the most expensive car she owns.
   B Eda doesn't love the car.

My hobby's collecting model cars. I started when I was quite young but I've never lost my passion for it. My friends think I'm crazy! My father had a few of his own and I used to play with them with my sister but for me it all really started when my cousin gave me a small model sportscar of my own for my ninth birthday.

I started small, saving my pocket money to buy cars for myself, and I reached 50 by the time I was 15. In the last few years my collection has grown from 100 to over 400.

I'm always looking for unusual cars or models that are rare. I sometimes go to sales, although they can be stressful, or wander through street markets, which I really love. It's very exciting when I see a car on a market stall that no one else realises is special and I can buy it at a good price. The most I've ever paid is £150 for a very rare car, which I'm glad I have but I don't love. One of my favourites only cost me £1. I don't want to sell any of my cars, though, I just love owning them and looking at them.

9 🎧 **L18** Look at the task. The student has got all the answers wrong. Listen to the recording and correct the mistakes they have made.

You hear this announcement about a local football club.

Players needed!

Minimum age for team: **(1)** _____ 15 _____
(2) _____ Some skill _____ not necessary
Training on Mondays from 7 to **(3)** _____ 9.30 _____
Membership cost: **(4)** £ _____ 5 _____
Team travel to away matches by **(5)** _____ car _____
For more information: www. **(6)** _____ footieco _____ .com

10 Look at the audioscript for Ex 9. Underline the correct answers. Why are they right?

We're looking for new players for our football team. You should be between 16 and 18, as we already have players for our over-19 and under-15 teams.

You don't need to have much experience, you just need to enjoy playing the game. Obviously we'd like people who have some skill but it's not the most important thing – that's having fun!

We play matches at the local stadium and train there, too. Our training takes place on Monday evenings, starting at 7 and finishing at 9. We always have a social get-together afterwards so no one leaves before 9:30.

We ask new players to join the club and there's a fee for that. It's only £45 a season but that doesn't include the match fee, which is £5 every home game, or any snacks – usually around £2. It does include the cost of travel to away matches though. We always go to those in a minibus so players don't have to use their own cars. If it's quite local, some fans sometimes go by bike!

If you're interested, go on to our website for more information – that's www.footyeco.com – f-o-o-t-y-e-c-o.com.

Checking grammar

> **TIP:** Make sure that your answer fits grammatically in the gap. This is a good way of checking that you have written the right word.

You must write the exact word you hear and you mustn't change it. The word you hear will always fit grammatically into the sentence.

11 🎧 **L19** Look at the sentences below and choose the correct answer to complete the sentences. Then listen and check your answers. Why is the other word incorrect?

1 All walkers should bring a **boots** / **towel** with them.

2 The friends enjoyed their trip to the **swimming** / **beach**.

3 My favourite food is **oranges** / **fruit**. It's delicious and good for me, too!

4 Alana thinks it's important for a goalkeeper to wear a **helmet** / **stick** when they play a hockey match.

5 Kit was delighted that the weather was **dry** / **rained** on her holiday.

6 You can see examples of Lucy's artwork on the college **magazine** / **website**.

L20 **For each question, write the correct answer in the gap.**

Write one or two words or a number or a date or a time.

You will hear a woman called Alina giving a presentation about a chocolate-making course she went on.

Alina's chocolate-making course

Alina's course was located in **(1)** _____ Restaurant.

Alina paid **(2)** £_____ for her course, which lasted two days.

The flavour of Alina's favourite dessert was **(3)** _____ .

Alina chose to make **(4)** _____ on the second day of the course.

Alina was surprised that the **(5)** _____ of chocolate is very important when you're making it.

More information about courses can be found at www.**(6)** _____ .com

ABOUT THE TASK

- In Listening Part 4, you hear one long interview. There are two speakers: an interviewer and an interviewee.
- You are told who is being interviewed and what they are talking about.
- There are six questions about the interview and three options (A, B and C) for each question. You choose the option which correctly answers the question.
- The questions come in the same order as the information you hear and each one is introduced by the interviewer.

- The questions test your understanding of the speaker's attitude, opinion and feelings, or a detail about what the speaker says.
- Some answers might focus on a phrase or sentence in the recording or you might need to understand the gist or main idea of what the speaker is saying.
- You have time to read the questions and options before you listen to the interview.
- There is one mark for each correct answer.

Practice task

1 🎧 **L21** For each question, choose the correct answer.

You will hear an interview with a woman called Joanna Winters who is talking about people's use of plastic.

1 Joanna protested against the use of plastic because
   A she was worried about how much of it she saw in the ocean.
   B she was annoyed about the way other people ignored it.
   C she was keen to join in with what other people were doing about it.

2 What does Joanna think about recycling plastic?
   A It's better to stop using it completely.
   B It's necessary to educate people about how to do it.
   C It's unlikely to solve the problem on its own.

3 How does Joanna feel about the future?
   A confused about how to pay for the changes needed
   B positive about changes that are already happening
   C confident about getting everyone involved in making changes

How did you do?

2a Look again at Ex 1 question 1. What is the question testing? Which words in the options A–C tell you?
   A opinion   B feeling   C detail

2b Read the audioscript for Ex 1 question 1. Underline the sentence(s) where Joanna gives her reason for protesting.

A: What made you protest against the use of plastic?
B: I was working on a documentary about marine life and when we were filming underwater there was lots of plastic around us. This made me anxious and I decided to make my own documentary about the problem, even though people said no one would watch it. It was my own individual protest really, but now plastic's become a hot topic and I'd like to think I played some part in that.

3a Look again at Ex 1 question 2. What is the question testing? Which word in the question tells you?
   A opinion   B feeling   C detail

3b Read the audioscript for Ex 1 question 2. Underline the sentence(s) that tell(s) you what her opinion is.

A: But we recycle a lot of plastic now so do you think that's helping?
B: It's a step forward but it's probably not good enough. I realise that we can't get rid of plastic completely, but we can certainly teach people more about the problems of single-use plastics and hopefully find alternative types of packaging for food and other goods. We have a long way to go with recycling but if you could see how much plastic there is in the oceans, you'd feel the same.

4a Look again at Ex 1 question 3. What is the question testing? Which word in the question tells you?
   A opinion   B feeling   C detail

4b You won't find a single word that tells you she feels positive, but you can find a general mood. Read the audioscript for Ex 1 question 3. Underline three phrases or sentences that show the speaker feels positive.

A: How do you feel about the future?
B: Although it's not totally clear, things are generally going in the right direction. The movement towards conservation and protecting the environment is growing, especially among young people, and unlike some businesses, they're not worried about any financial costs of reducing plastic. They'll find the way forward and their protests will be heard.

Strategies and skills

Listening for opinions

A speaker may not state their opinion clearly but you can still understand what they think.

1 Read the sentences below. What is the speaker's opinion in each case?

1 You can't be good at lots of different sports – it's much better to be really good at one.
   A It's a good idea to do fewer sports so that you can become an expert in one.
   B It's enjoyable to do lots of sports and it's not important to be good at one of them.

2 The hotel we stayed in was fantastic. It didn't matter that it was outside the town centre.
   A I liked the hotel even though it wasn't in a perfect location.
   B The location of the hotel was a problem for me.

3 The argument my friends had wasn't as serious as it looked and now everything's fine.
   A I think that the argument between my friends was a bad one.
   B I think my friends still have a good relationship.

4 I believe it's easier to solve problems if you talk about them with friends.
   A It's a good idea to talk about problems you have.
   B It's difficult to solve problems by talking about them.

5 There are many different reasons why it's important to protect the environment.
   A We need to know reasons why we should protect the environment.
   B We should all protect the environment for lots of reasons.

6 The best thing about history is what we can all learn from reading about it.
   A In my opinion, it's interesting to read about history.
   B History is important because we can learn from it.

2 🎧 **L22 Listen to students talking and decide whether the man or the woman has the opinion given.**

1 People rely on mobile phones more than they should. **Man / Woman**

2 It's important to think about the environment more than we do. **Man / Woman**

3 Listening to music isn't a good way to relax on a journey. **Man / Woman**

4 I don't have enough free time to follow my interests. **Man / Woman**

5 Being an actor must be a great job – I'd love to do it! **Man / Woman**

6 It's difficult to believe what people say on social media. **Man / Woman**

Discuss or answer.

1 What environmental issues do you feel most concerned about?

2 Can we use other planets to improve life on Earth? In what ways?

Identifying reasons

TIP: Speakers often use a phrase to introduce a reason for what they say or think. Listen for these phrases as they help you to identify the speaker's opinion.

3 🎧 **L23 Choose the best word or phrase to complete each sentence. Then listen and check your answers.**

1 Everyone should play a musical instrument **for example / because** it makes people feel happy.

2 We all know a lot more about wildlife **due to / for example** television documentaries.

3 My interests include bird-watching and wildlife photography **so / but** I choose to live in the countryside.

4 I'd love to sing on stage but the **reason / problem** is that I have a terrible voice!

5 The new film had great reviews and **that's why / that's because** I'm going to see it on Saturday.

6 I stayed up late last night and **that's the result / that's the reason** why I'm tired today.

7 I joined a gym **so that / when** I could get fit.

8 I usually study at the weekends **because / in order to** get a good grade at college.

Identifying the main idea

4 🎧 **L24 Listen to eight different people talking about shopping. What is their main idea? For each person, choose the correct answer, A or B.**

1 A Buying clothes without trying them on first is not sensible.
   B Buying clothes because they are cheap is not always a good idea.

2 A We spend too much money on buying new things.
   B We should keep things we buy for longer.

3 A People enjoy shopping too much.
   B It's difficult to know what to buy.

4 A The things people choose to spend money on have changed.
   B Young people don't have enough money to spend.

5 A There are too many advertisements on television.
   B We need to help children to understand advertisements.

6 A It's nicer to think about other people than yourself.
   B It's always fun to go shopping whatever you're buying.

7 A It's always better to buy things online.
   B Buying things in shops has other advantages.

8 A Shopping is tiring and stressful.
   B People go shopping for the wrong reason.

Recognising distractors

> **TIP:** You may hear ideas relevant to all the options but only one option will answer the question.

It's important to understand why two of the options are not the correct answer to each question.

5 **You will hear a man called Kyle talking about writing recipes for a living. Look at question 1 and the options (A–C). What are you listening for, A or B?**

A the reason Kyle started writing recipes

B how Kyle feels about writing recipes

---
1 Why did Kyle start writing recipes?
  A He liked reading about different kinds of food.
  B He wanted to recreate food he had eaten.
  C He was advised to do it by a friend.
---

6 🎧 **L25** **Read the audioscript for Ex 5 question 1 and answer the questions. Then listen and check your answers.**

1 Option A. Does Kyle say he started by reading recipes?

2 Option C. Does Kyle say his friend advised him to start writing recipes?

3 Option B. Does Kyle say that he wanted to cook meals he had eaten in other countries? Underline the sentence that tells you that.

I've always loved cooking but I've never wanted to be a chef – it's too stressful! After college I decided to see the world. I joined a travel company and it was great to have the chance to eat a real variety of food from different places. I made notes of unusual meals I had and wrote them down as recipes so that I could cook them for myself later. One day a friend suggested I send these to a food website. So I did and they offered me a job.
---

7 **Now look at question 2. What are you listening for, A or B?**

A Kyle's opinion of his job

B Kyle's feelings about his job

---
2 Kyle thinks that in his job
  A it's useful to come up with fresh ideas.
  B it's important to encourage people to experiment with food.
  C it's necessary to make cooking easy for people who try his recipes.
---

8 🎧 **L26** **The answer to Ex 7 question 2 is C. Listen and decide why A and B are not correct.**

9 **Now look at question 3. What are you listening for, A or B?**

A What Kyle does every day in his work

B What Kyle likes best about his work

---
3 What does Kyle enjoy most about his job?
  A producing a successful recipe
  B planning recipes with other people
  C choosing a picture for every recipe
---

10 🎧 **L27** **The answer to Ex 9 question 3 is A. Listen and decide why B and C are not correct.**

🎧 **L28** **For each question, choose the correct answer.**

You will hear an interview with Carrie Silver, a young writer who has become famous for her poetry.

1 Carrie thinks that what makes poetry special for her is
A the message she is able to give.
B the memory of her mum reading.
C the sound different words make.

2 What does Carrie say about her career?
A She didn't plan it.
B She wanted to make money.
C She finds it hard to compete with others.

3 When she's writing poetry, Carrie feels
A confident about her own ability.
B confused about friends' criticism.
C surprised about how long it takes her.

4 What does Carrie say about the way she writes poetry?
A It's impossible to think of something new every time.
B Writing the final version is the best part.
C There's too much pressure sometimes.

5 How does Carrie feel about writing a play?
A happy about the schedule
B pleased to be part of a team
C satisfied with her script

6 What advice does Carrie give to other young writers?
A Read as much as you can.
B Contact your favourite writers.
C Develop your own style.

ABOUT THE TASK

- In Speaking Part 1, the examiner asks you and your partner individual questions about yourselves. There are two phases to this part.

- In Phase 1, the questions are very easy and factual – your name, where you come from or live and what you do. You only need to give short answers to these questions.

- In Phase 2, the examiner asks you questions about things such as your hobbies, what you like or don't like, what you like to do with your friends and so on. You should give longer answers to these questions.

- You should not talk to your partner in this part of the test.

- Use this part to relax and start to enjoy the test.

Practice task

1 🎧 **S01** **Read these Speaking Part 1 questions. Then listen and answer the questions yourself.**

What's your name?

Where do you come from?

Do you work or are you a student?

What do you do/study?

What do you like doing in your free time?

What did you do yesterday?

Is there a city you would like to visit in the future?

Do you use social media very often?

How did you do?

2 **Look at the Part 1 questions again and some student answers (A–C). Choose the best answer for each question.**

1 What's your name?
   - **A** My name is Caroline but my friends call me Caro.
   - **B** Caroline.
   - **C** My partner's name is Caroline.

2 Where do you come from?
   - **A** Paris.
   - **B** Paris, which is in northern France.
   - **C** I live in Paris.

3 Do you work or are you a student?
   - **A** I'm a student.
   - **B** Student.
   - **C** I enjoy being a student.

4 What do you do/study?
   - **A** I study English at college.
   - **B** I like to study English.
   - **C** English.

5 What do you like doing in your free time?
   - **A** Playing tennis.
   - **B** I like playing any sport, especially tennis.
   - **C** I think tennis is a really good game.

6 What did you do yesterday?
   - **A** I went to the cinema.
   - **B** I usually go to the cinema at the weekend.
   - **C** I went to the cinema yesterday and watched a film about the future.

7 Is there a city you would like to visit in the future?
   - **A** I went to New York last year.
   - **B** I think I would like to visit New York.
   - **C** New York.

8 Do you use social media very often?
   - **A** It depends, but usually every day.
   - **B** What is social media?
   - **C** No.

3 🎧 **S02** **Listen and check your answers.**

4 **Think about the other answers in Ex 2. Choose the best reason why each of these answers is not so good.**
   - It doesn't answer the question.
   - It is too simple.

5 🎧 **S03** **Listen again. Think about your own answers to the questions in Ex 1. Answer the questions below.**

Did you:
   - answer the questions?
   - give interesting answers and not just simple ones?

6 🎧 **S04** **Listen to the questions in Ex 1 again. Answer them using the checklist in Ex 5.**

Strategies and skills
Answering questions

> **TIP:** In the exam, you should start your answer to a question as naturally as possible. Your answer does not have to repeat any of the question. For example:
> **Q:** What are you studying at the moment?
> **A:** ~~I'm studying~~ science and technology and I'm enjoying both subjects very much.

1 **Cross out the unnecessary part of the answers below to make them sound more natural.**

1 Where do you live?
I live in Genoa, in Italy.

2 What do you usually do in the evenings?
In the evenings I usually chat to my friends online.

3 What's your favourite sport?
My favourite sport is definitely football because I love team sports.

4 How often do you look at your mobile phone?
I look at my mobile phone probably every ten minutes or so!

5 What did you do last weekend?
Last weekend I went to the beach with my family.

6 Who is your best friend?
My best friend is Julia – I've known her for years as she lives next door to me.

2 **S05 Listen and check your answers.**

3 **Match questions 1-6 with answers A-F.**

1 Do you work or are you a student?

2 How often do you go to the cinema?

3 Where do you usually meet your friends?

4 Are you good at sport?

5 Do you go on holiday abroad every year?

6 Do you have many brothers and sisters?

A Every weekend if I can.

B I work. I'm a teacher at a college.

C Different places. For example, the local café or the shopping mall.

D Not always, but most years.

E No, I don't think so, to be honest.

F No, just one brother.

Giving reasons

> **TIP:** If you practise adding 'because' or a similar word to your answer so that you give a reason, this will help you to say more.

4 **Which word or phrase below <u>can't</u> be used to give a reason?**

- as
- the main reason is
- after that
- because
- so

5 **Rewrite the sentences using the words and phrases from Ex 4.**

1 The reason I like films is I think they're fun.
I like films _____ I think they're fun.

2 The reason I haven't visited other countries is I don't have time.
I don't have much time _____ I haven't visited other countries.

3 I need to practise my music more but it's not easy.
I don't practise my music more _____ it's not easy.

4 I can't get to college because my car has broken down.
The _____ I can't get to college is my car has broken down.

6 **Look at the questions below. What extra information could you add to the answers? Complete the answers with your own ideas.**

1 **A:** How do you travel to work every day? (Why?)
B: By bus because _____ .

2 **A:** Do you like going out in the evening? (Why?)
B: I do as _____ .

3 **A:** Do you have a lot of free time during the week?
B: Not much.
A: Why not?
B: I work hard so _____ .

4 **A:** Do you usually prefer to travel by bus or by car? (Why?)
B: By car as it's _____ .

5 **A:** What's your favourite kind of television programme? (Why?)
B: I really like _____ as _____ .

6 **A:** Do you ever go to the theatre?
B: Not very often.
A: Why not?
B: The main reason is _____ .

Adding information to your answer

> **TIP:** You should answer the question you're asked but try to make your answers interesting by adding extra information.

You can add details or examples to your answers.

7 **Complete the table with the words in the box.**

> also   and   as well as   for example
> for instance   like   on top of that   such as

giving more details	giving examples

8 For each answer, choose the correct word/phrase to add information.

1 I love doing things at the weekend – **for example** / **when** I play tennis if the weather's good.

2 I listen to classical music **such as** / **as well as** rock and pop.

3 I often go to watch musical films, **such as** / **also** 'La La Land'.

4 I enjoy films about history, **like** / **so as** 'Elizabeth'.

5 I'm good at singing **as well as** / **and** my teacher wants me to take some exams.

6 Let's eat at the Indian restaurant tonight. The food's good and **also** / **for example** there's live music!

7 I'm good at team sports, **for instance** / **and** basketball.

9 Complete the answers below so that they are true for you. Give extra information or examples to make your answers interesting.

1 At the best party I've ever been to we danced and on top of that we _____ .

2 My favourite kind of film is _____ , for example _____ .

3 I'm really good at _____ and _____ .

4 I once went on an adventure break where I did rock climbing and as well as that I _____ .

5 I enjoyed my last holiday when we _____ and we also _____ .

6 I would really like to visit a Spanish- speaking country such as _____ .

Using interesting language

> **TIP:** Try not to repeat words too often so that you use a range of language to show the examiner what you can do.

10 Replace the underlined words with the words in the box to make the sentences more interesting.

> angry   boring   bought   comfortable   enjoyable
> fantastic   finally   hate   love   prefer   visited

1 I like listening to music but I <u>like</u> _____ playing my guitar <u>more</u>.

2 I <u>really don't like</u> _____ people making lots of noise – it makes me <u>feel bad</u> _____ .

3 I <u>really like</u> _____ listening to birds singing.

4 Last year I stayed in a <u>really nice</u> _____ hotel. It had very <u>nice</u> _____ beds so I slept well.

5 It was difficult to find a birthday present for my brother. <u>After a long time</u> _____ I <u>got</u> _____ him a video game.

6 I watched a film last night. After that I <u>went to see</u> _____ my friend in town.

7 It's <u>not interesting</u> _____ spending all day talking to friends online – meeting them in person is more <u>interesting</u> _____ .

Asking the examiner to repeat

> **TIP:** Remember that the examiner can only repeat the question. They can't use different words or explain what they mean.

If you have not heard a question correctly, you can ask the examiner to repeat it.

11 Match 1–6 with A–F to make phrases you can use to ask the examiner to repeat the question.

1	I'm sorry but could	A	did you say, please?
2	Would you mind	B	you say that again, please?
3	I'm not sure what	C	repeat that, please?
4	Sorry, I didn't hear	D	repeating the question, please?
5	Sorry, but what	E	what you said.
6	Could you	F	you said, I'm sorry.

If you don't understand a question, it's better to say so. The examiner will then ask you a different question. It's not a good idea to give an answer that is completely wrong.

12 Complete the phrases with the words in the box.

> anything   idea   mean   sure   understand   what

1 I'm sorry, I don't _____ the question.

2 I'm not _____ what you're asking me.

3 I don't know what you _____ .

4 I have no _____ about that, I'm sorry.

5 I don't know _____ to say.

6 I can't say _____ about that I'm afraid.

EXAM TASK

🎧 **S06** Listen to the questions. Answer them so that they are true for you.

Phase 1

What's your name?

Where do you live/come from?

Do you work or are you a student?

What do you do/study?

Phase 2

What do you have for breakfast every day?

What did you do last weekend?

What job would you like to do in the future?

Tell us about your favourite sport.

🎧 **S07** There is an example answer provided.

ABOUT THE TASK

- In Speaking Part 2, you talk by yourself for about a minute. You should not help your partner or interrupt them when they are speaking in this part.
- The examiner gives you a photograph, tells you what the situation is and asks you to talk about it.
- The photograph shows an everyday situation, for example at home, at work, on holiday. There are always people in the photograph.

- You need to describe what you can see in the photograph as well as what the people are doing.
- You should try to organise your talk logically and link your ideas clearly.
- Although you need vocabulary to describe what you can see in your photograph, don't worry if you don't know a particular word.
- The examiner stops you after about a minute and gives your partner a different photograph to talk about.

Practice task

1 **S08** Look at the photograph and listen to the instructions. Complete the task. If possible, record your answer so that you can listen to it again.

> Now I'd like each of you to talk on your own about something. I'm going to give each of you a photograph and I'd like you to talk about it.
>
> Student A, here is your photograph. It shows people cooking at home.
>
> Please tell us what you can see in the photograph.

How did you do?

2 **S09** Listen to two students (A and B) doing the task and answer the questions for each one.

1 Did they talk about everything in the photograph?
2 Did they speak fluently or did they hesitate?
3 Did they link their ideas clearly?
4 Were there any words they didn't know? Was this a problem?

3 Which student gave the better answer? Why?

4 Think about your own answer to the task, or listen to it again. Answer the questions below.

Did you:
- talk about everything in the photograph?
- speak fluently?
- link your ideas clearly?
- talk for about a minute?

5 Look at the photograph. It shows people eating at home. Talk about the photograph using the checklist in Ex 4 to help you.

6 **S10** Listen to an example response to the task. Did you talk about similar things? What could you have done better?

TEACH

Strategies and skills
Speaking fluently

> **TIP:** If you are not sure exactly what you want to say and need to think for a moment, it's better not to be silent while you think. This can seem hesitant. There are expressions (called fillers) that you can say while you think.

1 **Match 1-5 with A-E to make expressions you can use while you think.**

1	I'm not	**A**	me think.
2	Erm, let	**B**	difficult.
3	Just	**C**	sure what to say.
4	It's	**D**	else can I say?
5	So what	**E**	a minute.

> **TIP:** It helps you to speak more fluently if you use expressions of place to make it clear what you are talking about. This also helps you to feel more confident and to organise your description in a logical way.

2 **Label the parts of the photograph with the phrases in the box.**

> at the top   in the background
> in the bottom left-hand corner
> in the middle   in the top right-hand corner

3 **Complete the sentences about the photograph with the words and phrases in the box.**

> all over   behind   between   in   looking at
> on each side   on the left   on the right   to   too

1 The family are spending time at home _____ their kitchen.

2 The father is standing _____ the two girls.

3 The girls are sitting _____ of him.

4 The girl _____ is wearing a striped T-shirt and she has long hair. She's _____ some papers.

5 The girl _____ is younger but she also has long hair and she is wearing a T-shirt, _____ . She's looking up at her father.

6 _____ the family I can see a cooker and other kitchen things such as cupboards.

7 There are some papers _____ the table and they are all working on them.

8 The father's holding a pen or pencil and he's pointing _____ something so I think he's helping the girls with their homework.

> **TIP:** It is a good idea to start your description with a sentence giving the general situation in the photograph. This is usually repeating what the examiner tells you in the task.

4 **Which sentence in Ex 3 is the overview sentence?**

TIP: Don't worry if you don't know a specific word – just move on or use a phrase to talk about it.

You may not know all the words you need to describe the photograph you are given but this is not a problem. There are phrases you can use if you are not sure of a word.

5 Complete the sentences with the words and phrases in the box.

can't remember   know   not sure   what's

1   I _____ the word for this but I just can't think of it at the moment.

2   I want to talk about that thing in the right-hand corner – _____ the word for it?

3   I'm _____ about it, but I think it's called a vase.

4   I know it's something you ride on but I _____ the name.

6 Look at the photograph. It shows a family having a picnic. Match the sentences with what they are describing in the photograph and write the name.

1   It's something you use to protect yourself from the sun or to sleep in. It's a _____ .

2   It's a kind of top we wear when the weather's hot. It's a _____ .

3   It's a place inland where there's water. It's a _____ .

4   It's something that you use to drink from. It's a _____ .

5   It's a container you can use to take water with you when you travel. It's a _____ .

6   It's a meal of lettuce, tomatoes and other cold food. It's a _____ .

7 🎧 **S11** **Listen to a student talking about the photograph below. Complete the overview sentence he uses.**

The photograph shows people _____ .

8 🎧 **S12** **Listen again and tick the expressions he uses in his description.**

- I can't remember the word.
- a kind of …
- It's something you use for …
- I'm not sure what it's called.
- So what else can I say?
- in the background …
- in the middle …
- on the left …
- on the right …

Linking ideas

9 Look at the photograph and instructions. Read the student's description and choose the best word to link the ideas in the sentences.

> Student A, here is your photograph. It shows friends studying together.
>
> Please tell us what you can see in the photograph.

I can see two friends studying together. They're sitting outside on the grass **¹so / and** they're working together – **²on the other hand / perhaps** they're doing their homework or helping each other to finish a project. The man on the right is wearing a checked shirt and brown trousers **³and / because** he's showing his friend something he's written in a notebook. They're **⁴also / both** smiling about it. The man on the left is wearing a yellow sweatshirt, blue jeans and striped trainers. He has headphones round his neck **⁵with / so** I guess he's listening to music **⁶during / while** he's working. There's also a laptop open in front of him so he's probably using that to do his work. Behind the two friends I can see a building which may be their college.

10 🎧 S13 **Listen and check your answers.**

11 Look at the photograph and instructions. Complete the student's description with the words in the box.

> and   anyway   because/as   but   so

> Student B, here is your photograph. It shows people spending a weekend at the seaside.
>
> Please tell us what you can see in the photograph.

I can see people who are spending a weekend at the seaside – I think it's a family **(1)** _____
I can see a mother, father and three children. On the right-hand side I can see a tent **(2)** _____
I guess that means that they're camping. In front of the tent there's a basket which probably has food in it. On the left of the photograph the sisters are running up from the beach **(3)** _____ they're carrying a bucket – maybe they've been collecting stones or shells. I don't think the weather is hot **(4)** _____ everyone is wearing warm clothes. The father's wearing a blue sweatshirt and I think the others are wearing coats or jackets. I don't know exactly what the father is doing **(5)** _____ maybe he's preparing to have a barbecue. They all look happy **(6)** _____ .

What to describe/giving a description

> **TIP:** When you are given your photograph, notice what you can talk about easily at first and what you can give more details about later.

12 **Look at the photograph on the right. Choose the best thing(s) to say first about the photograph using the questions 1–4.**

1 Where are the people? **park / street / countryside / garden**

2 How do you know? **trees / fence / people in the background / traffic lights**

3 How many people are there? How do they look? **bored / happy / excited**

4 What are they doing? **walking / cycling / running / talking**

13 **Now think about more details to include in your description. Make notes in the table.**

clothes	
weather	
details about the place	
details about the people	

14 **Look at the words in the box below that you could use in a description of the photograph. Put them in the correct column in the table in Ex 13. There are some words that you can't use for this photograph.**

> black jacket   blue shirt   cars
> dogs   fence   green sweater
> lamppost   long hair   jeans   path
> rain   rubbish bins   scarf
> short hair   spotted shirt   sunny
> tall trees   trainers   wooden house

15 **S14 Listen to a student talking about the photograph. Tick the words in Ex 14 she uses.**

16 **S15 Another student has described the same photograph but has made six mistakes. Read what the student said and correct the mistakes. Then listen and see if you were right.**

I can see three women cycling in a park. The woman on the left is wearing a blue shirt and a scarf, while the woman on the left is wearing a dark jacket. They are all wearing casual clothes so they must be just having fun together and they are all looking happy. Two women have long hair and all the bicycles are red and one is blue. In the background I can see some trees and a lamppost in the middle of the picture. It looks sunny and warm. There are some other people in front of the cyclists but they're walking through the park, not cycling.

17 **Look at the photograph. It shows friends relaxing in the evening. Talk about it for a minute and record yourself if possible.**

🎧 **S16 Listen and complete the exam task.**

Candidate A, here is your photograph. It shows **people having a music lesson**.

Please tell us what you can see in the photograph.

Candidate B, here is your photograph. It shows **people waiting to travel at an airport**.

Please tell us what you can see in the photograph.

🎧 **S17 There is an example answer provided.**

ABOUT THE TASK

- In Speaking Part 3, you discuss something with your partner for about two minutes.
- The examiner describes a situation and gives you a picture with some ideas for you to talk about.
- The situation may be something like choosing a present for a teacher or planning an activity to do with friends. You discuss this situation with your partner and make a decision about it.

- In your discussion, you should give your own opinion and ask your partner what they think.
- The examiner stops you after two minutes. It doesn't matter if you haven't made a decision in this time.

Practice task

1 🎧 **S18 Look at the pictures and listen to the examiner giving students the task.**

> Now, in this part of the test you're going to talk about something together for about two minutes. I'm going to describe a situation to you.
>
> A young man wants to do a new sport to help him keep fit but he doesn't have a lot of time.
>
> Here are some things he could do.
>
> Talk together about the different sports he could do, and say which would be best.

2 Make notes of things you could say about each sport. Think about why each one would be a good or a bad idea for the young man to do.

How did you do?

3 🎧 **S19 Listen to two students doing the task. Did they have similar ideas to yours?**

4 🎧 **S20 Listen again to the students doing the task. Answer the questions.**

Do they:

1 discuss all the prompts? If not, which one(s) do they not discuss?
2 ask each other what they think?
3 give their own opinions?
4 give reasons for their opinions?
5 decide what is the best thing for the young man to do?

5 🎧 **S21 Listen again. Tick all the phrases you hear the students use to ask for their partner's opinion and to say what they think themselves.**

What about … ?   Do you like … ?
Do you think … ?   I prefer …
Any ideas about … ?   In my opinion …
I don't like it much.   I don't think … is a good idea.
What do you think about … ?   I don't agree because …

6 🎧 **S22 The students give reasons for their opinions. Listen again and answer the questions.**

1 Why does the woman not recommend rock climbing?
  A It's expensive.
  B He can't do it on his own.
  C It's difficult to learn.
2 Why do they both like the idea of swimming?
  A There are lots of courses.
  B It's fun.
  C It's a good way to keep fit.
3 Why does the man recommend running?
  A There's not much to learn.
  B It doesn't take time.
  C It's a good way to keep fit.

7 Think about your own answers to Ex 2 again, or repeat the task. Answer the questions below.

Did you:
- give your own opinion?
- ask for your partner's opinion?
- give a reason for your opinion?
- reach a decision?

Strategies and skills

Making suggestions and recommendations

> **TIP:** Try to use different language to make suggestions and recommendations.

1 Read the exam task and put the words in the correct order to make suggestions.

> A young woman has got a new job and is going to live in another city. She wants to know what she could do to make her new life in the city easier and more enjoyable.

1 She / become / should / a / of / member / running / a / club / .

2 She / go / a / college / on / course / at / could / a / local / .

3 How / joining / about / gym / a / ?

4 I / that / she / a / starts / new / suggest / hobby / .

5 She / buy / a / bike / could / the / to / explore / city / .

6 What / car / learning / about / drive / a / to / ?

7 I / that / she / the / recommend / walks / city / with / her / camera / around / .

8 She / to / possible / has / try / make / to / new / as / soon / friends / as / .

It's important to give a reason for your suggestion or recommendation.

2 Match the reasons (A-H) with the suggestions (1-8) in Ex 1.

A It will give her a new interest.

B Then she can make friends with the other members.

C Then she can drive home and visit old friends where she used to live.

D That's a good way to keep fit and she can use the equipment there.

E If she doesn't do that, she might feel lonely.

F She can go further than on foot and find new places to visit.

G Then she can take photos of interesting places.

H She can meet people there and a course can be useful, too.

3 🎧 **S23** Listen to two students discussing the situation. Which three of the suggestions (1-5) do they make? Which of the reasons (A-E) do they give for each of their suggestions?

1 Join a club.   A It's healthy.

2 Use social media.   B They're interesting to visit.

3 Talk to neighbours.   C You won't be lonely.

4 Take up a sport.   D It's a good way to meet people.

5 Go to museums.   E You have friends to talk to online.

Asking for opinions

In Speaking Part 3, you should ask your partner for their opinions as well as giving your own.

4 Look at the expressions below. Put them into the correct column and add question marks where necessary.

- Do you think that …
- How about …
- I think …
- In my opinion …
- My view on this is …
- What do you think …

asking for your partner's opinion	giving your own opinion

Agreeing and disagreeing

5 **Look at the phrases below. Which agree and which disagree? Write A or D for each one.**

1 I'm sure you're right.
2 That's a good point.
3 I have a different idea.
4 I don't think you're quite right.
5 That's not what I think.
6 That could be a good idea.
7 I think the same.
8 I'm not sure about that.
9 Me, too.
10 Sorry, I don't think so.

6 🎧 **S24 Listen to the dialogues. Tick the phrases from Ex 5 that you hear.**

Discussing and making a decision

> **TIP:** The examiner will stop you after two minutes. Your discussion is more important than the decision you do or don't make so don't worry if you don't have time to reach a conclusion.

When you try to make a decision about what is best or more interesting, you must discuss it together. You should ask each other what you think and check that you agree with each other's decision.

7 **Match the sentence beginnings (1–8) with the endings (A–H).**

1 How do you
2 Do you think
3 So do we
4 Shall we
5 I'd like to choose
6 I like the idea of the pen,
7 Is that
8 I think

A the book, if you agree.
B both think the same?
C feel about my idea?
D OK?
E choose that one?
F that's best.
G don't you?
H the same as me?

When you have made a decision you should state this clearly.

8 **Complete the decisions below with the words in the box.**

> because best both choice choose chosen
> decided should thing useful

1 Let's _____ your idea – it's the _____ one.
2 So we _____ think that the saucepan is the most _____ .
3 We agree that he _____ buy the book.
4 So we've _____ that the camera is the best gift.
5 The pen is our _____ _____ we think he'll use it a lot.
6 We've _____ the camera, which is the cheapest _____ for him to buy.

S25 Listen and complete the exam task.

A young man wants to give his parents a present for their 25th wedding anniversary. He doesn't have much money to spend but he wants his parents to feel special.

Here are some things he could give his parents.

Talk together about the things he could give his parents and say which would be best.

 S26 There is an example answer provided.

TEST

ABOUT THE TASK

- In Speaking Part 4, the examiner asks you and your partner some questions. These questions are connected to the topic you have already discussed in Part 3.

- After your partner has answered a question, the examiner may ask you if you agree with what your partner has said. So you must always listen to your partner and think about what you could say.

- There is no right answer to any of the questions so you should just say what you think. Try to give full answers if you can.

- You can also discuss the examiner's question with your partner if you want to.

Practice task

TIP: The topic of the questions in Part 4 is always connected to the topic of Part 3. For example, if you have been talking about holidays in Part 3, the examiner asks you some more questions about holidays in Part 4.

1 🎧 **S27 Read and listen to the questions. Make notes on what you would say in answer to each question.**

1 Do you usually buy presents for friends when you go on holiday?

2 Do you buy many holiday souvenirs for yourself?

3 Is it always important to spend a lot of money on a present for someone else?

4 Have you ever made a present for someone instead of buying a present for them?

5 Do you think it's more enjoyable to give a present to someone else or to receive one yourself?

How did you do?

2 🎧 **S28 Listen to two students giving their own answers to the questions. Were their ideas similar to yours?**

3 🎧 **S29 Listen to the answer to question 1 in Ex 1 again. Does Juan give a reason for his opinion? What is it?**

A I don't like wasting time on holiday.

B It's always important to buy presents for people.

4 🎧 **S30 Listen to the answer to question 2 in Ex 1 again. Does Maria give a personal example of her experience? What is it?**

A buying something useful to wear

B spending a long time buying something

5 Look at what the two students said for question 3 in Ex 1. Underline the phrases they use to introduce their opinion.

Examiner:	Is it always important to spend a lot of money on a present for someone else?
Maria:	I'm not sure about that. I think it's nice to spend a lot of money but only if I'm sure that the person will like it. In my opinion it's a mistake to spend a lot of money on something they might not like!
Examiner:	What do you think, Juan?
Juan:	I agree with Maria. Personally, I believe that it's important to spend more money if it's a special birthday or anniversary present. It doesn't matter if it's not a special occasion.

6 Look at what Maria said for question 4 in Ex 1. Underline two phrases she uses to give examples.

I don't do that very often but I have done it sometimes, like when I wanted to give someone a special present. For example, I made a book of photographs for my mother. Another thing I did was I painted a card for my grandmother. She liked that!

7 🎧 **S31 Listen again to what the students said for question 5 in Ex 1. Choose the correct option, A or B.**

1 What reason does Maria give for why she likes giving presents?

A She likes to see someone happy.

B She likes choosing presents.

2 Does Juan agree or disagree with her? What reason does he give?

A He likes having lots of things.

B He likes having a surprise.

Strategies and skills

Describing opinions, likes and dislikes

In the exam, you have to give your opinion or say what you like, dislike or prefer.

1 Complete the table with the phrases in the box.

> I can't stand   I don't like   I (really) enjoy   I find that   I hate
> I love   I'm fond of   I'm not keen on   I prefer   I think that
> It seems to me that   Personally, I believe that

introducing opinions	saying what you like	saying what you dislike

2 🎧 **S32** **Listen to two students talking about their college. Tick the phrases they use from Ex 1.**

Giving examples and personal experiences

You should try to give an example to support your opinion.

3 Complete the sentences with the words in the box.

> example   including   like   such

1   Some people try to look after the environment – for _____ , they cycle instead of driving a car.

2   I like watching different kinds of films, _____ as adventure films and musicals.

3   It's good to do activities on holiday – things _____ hiking or swimming.

4   I hate seeing any kind of rubbish on the ground, _____ paper.

4 Choose the best word (A, B or C) to complete each sentence.

1   My friends love jazz, but _____ for myself, I prefer rock music.
    A speaking   B talking   C saying

2   Things always happen when I go shopping – like _____ , I lost my purse and had to walk home!
    A sometimes   B once   C usually

3   I love action films and I really like it _____ there is a car chase.
    A even   B when   C though

4   It was a great party! _____ me tell you about it.
    A Can   B Shall   C Let

5   I had a lot of fun and _____ is why – all my friends were there.
    A what   B this   C which

6   I'd like to give you one _____ of why I love tennis – I can hit the ball really hard.
    A example   B idea   C suggestion

7   I love seeing new cities – I _____ one visit to Florence a few years ago where we saw so many interesting places.
    A remind   B know   C remember

Giving reasons

> **TIP:** If you give a reason for your opinion, you can use a variety of language.

5 Match the opinions (1–6) with the reasons (A–F).

1   I think it's easier to stay healthy by eating good food than by doing exercise. That's because

2   I feel we don't recycle enough. The reason is

3   It seems to me that all young children should do sport as

4   I believe that everyone should turn off their mobile phone for an hour a day. My reason is

5   I find that it's easier to study in the mornings. That's when

6   In my opinion, it's good to listen to music in the evening because

A   we all spend too much time looking at screens.
B   people don't think it's important to do it.
C   it's a good way for them to keep fit.
D   it's more relaxing than using a computer.
E   meals are nice and exercise isn't.
F   I can concentrate on my work.

EXAM TASK

🎧 **S33** **Imagine that in Part 3 of the Speaking test you have been talking about activities families can do together to relax. Now the examiner asks you some further questions about the topic. Listen to the questions. Answer them so they are true for you.**

What do you usually do when you want to relax? (Why?)

Do you think watching sport is relaxing? (Why? / Why not?)

Do you sometimes choose to do nothing in the evenings or do you always like to be busy? (Why?)

If you're on holiday, do you prefer to do lots of sightseeing or to take it easy? (Why?)

Do you think it's important to turn off your mobile phone sometimes so that you can relax? (Why? / Why not?)

🎧 **S34** **There is an example answer provided.**

TEST

Questions 1–5

For each question, choose the correct answer.

1

> Chloe,
>
> I've got to finish some homework before I go to school tomorrow and I'm terrible at getting up. Could you wake me at 6:30 in the morning? I'll catch the bus instead of walking.
>
> Jan

A Jan wants Chloe to help her with some homework.
B Jan wants Chloe to drive her to school.
C Jan wants Chloe to stop her sleeping too late.

2

> Do you want regular information about our new college courses? Fill in the form with your contact details and email.

A You can't come on a new college course unless you have completed the form.
B You must complete the form to receive emails about courses starting at the college.
C You need to email the college to get the form to complete before joining their courses.

3

> Ten percent discount for anyone buying more than five books. Five percent discount for students on all items. (ID necessary.)

A All students with ID can get a five percent discount on everything.
B Students with ID must buy more than five books to save money.
C Anyone can ask for a discount of five percent if they have ID.

4

> **To:** Tom   **From:** Marc
>
> Hi Tom,
>
> Any chance of playing tennis tomorrow afternoon?
> I thought I was meeting Joe then but he's just texted
> to say he's got to visit his grandmother. See you at the
> club at 6?
>
> Marc

A   Marc wants Tom to send a message to Joe.
B   Marc wants Tom to meet him the next day.
C   Marc wants Tom to visit a family member with him.

5

> **Ice on the road ahead.**
> **Driving difficult until early evening.**
> **Take great care.**

A   You have just passed a difficult part of the road.
B   The road ahead is too dangerous to drive on.
C   Be careful when driving on the road during the day.

Questions 6–10

For each question, choose the correct answer.

The people below all want to visit towns.

On the opposite page there are descriptions of eight towns.

Decide which place would be most suitable for the people below.

6

Jon is hoping to find a special present for his grandmother's birthday. He also wants to visit a photography exhibition and is interested in going to the cinema in the evening.

7

Ali wants to take her children to do some water sports and have a picnic in a park with them afterwards. She doesn't drive so needs to have good public transport.

8

Cris wants to take a guided tour of the town before eating at a famous restaurant. He'd like to go to the theatre in the evening.

9

Susie would like to go to watch a sports game with some friends. She wants to go to a music concert in the evening and needs to stay overnight in cheap accommodation.

10

Wang loves art, particularly traditional painting, so he wants to see some while he's there. He's also keen on architecture and would like to see some interesting old buildings. He'd like to buy some clothes while he's there.

Different towns

A

Barnsville

This historic seaside town is full of fascinating houses built in different styles. One of the oldest of these now has collections of modern and traditional art and another holds music concerts and plays. It's not all culture because there's a modern shopping centre selling the latest fashions and a huge football stadium for sports fans to visit.

B

Appledown

You can swim in the sea or in the pool and spend time enjoying the gardens and open spaces. It's a popular resort so you should book your hotel early to avoid paying high prices. There are often exhibitions in the local museum, which are interesting for adults and children alike. It has a shop for gifts and a café for snacks.

C

Anderstown

The large arts and crafts market in the town centre sells perfect gifts. The town has a long history and there are daily tours of the most interesting areas. These start at the town hall, where there's also an exhibition of old black and white photographs of the town. For anyone who likes films there's a new entertainment complex showing the latest blockbusters.

D

Lambton

This small town has a fascinating history. You can walk round with a knowledgeable guide and explore the old streets and buildings, one of which has a well-known place to eat on the top floor. For those less interested in history there's an entertainment centre where you can see plays by new writers. Why not stay in one of our luxurious hotels?

E

Dunmount

If you're interested in art, then this is the place for you. There are three galleries to choose from, including one that specialises in photography. There are good bus connections between them so you can do them all in a day before relaxing at one of the theatres or concert halls. For sports fans there is an excellent leisure centre and pool to enjoy.

F

Newcome

You won't be bored here! It's full of open spaces perfect for eating outside and beautiful gardens to walk through. It's by the sea so you can hire a boat and there are two swimming pools offering different activities for all ages. Cars aren't allowed in the centre so there's an excellent bus service if you have shopping to carry!

G

Cambton

Famous for its football team, there's a great match most weekends and a whole museum for the history of the team. There's so much to do here that many people stay overnight as the hotels are reasonably priced and comfortable. You'll find great entertainment, including bands performing in the theatre regularly. Why not try some of the excellent food on offer at the various restaurants?

H

Harsten

Need to buy a gift? No problem! Here you can find the perfect things for a relative or friend. And while you're here why not buy yourself something to wear in one of the department stores? If anyone in your group gets bored while you shop, then leave them to watch a film or go to the local sports stadium to watch a game.

Questions 11–15

For each question, choose the correct answer.

Andy Thompson describes how he first learnt to dive

I was on holiday and feeling rather bored. My family were all enjoying lying on the beach, but I wanted something more exciting to do that I hadn't done before. I thought about fishing or water-skiing but when I saw an advert for diving lessons for beginners it looked like the perfect solution, even though it did seem rather expensive. When I told them my plan, my family worried about how safe it was but I did some quick research online and discovered that if you are sensible and follow the rules, it's as safe as anything else.

The course lasted two days. On the first day we had to meet at the swimming pool rather than on the beach, which I hadn't expected. Then I realised it was because we had to learn the basics before we could go into the sea. The instructor, Jenny, said the most important thing for a diver was not to be really good at swimming but to be able to move around comfortably in the water, and that was why we were going to spend the first day in the pool.

There were only four of us so it was obvious that we'd get lots of individual attention. Jenny showed us the equipment and explained how to use it and although it looked complicated, I got used to it pretty quickly. I really wanted to get out and explore the underwater world immediately but we spent all day doing different exercises in the pool until we felt totally confident about being underwater. I'm a good swimmer but one person on the course was very nervous and needed a lot of help.

On the second day we went into the sea. The boat stayed close to shore and before we went in Jenny reminded us of everything we had learnt and put us into pairs so we could help each other. The water was incredibly clear and we were surrounded by groups of fish almost immediately. It was fascinating and I couldn't believe my eyes. I had so much to tell my family afterwards! I'll definitely go diving again.

11 Why did Andy decide to take the diving course?
  A to please his family
  B to have a new experience
  C to do something dangerous
  D to take advantage of a special offer

12 What surprised Andy on the first day of the course?
  A where they had to meet
  B the special skills a diver needed
  C how important it was to be a good swimmer
  D how short the course was

13 What annoyed Andy about being in the pool?
  A the type of practice exercises they had to do there
  B how difficult the equipment there was to use
  C what kind of advice he was given there
  D how long he had to spend there before going in the sea

14 How did Andy feel after diving in the sea?
  A proud of what he had done
  B happy that nothing had gone wrong
  C amazed by what he had seen
  D sad that his family had not been with him

15 What might a member of his family say about Andy's experience of learning to dive?

  A He enjoyed it and recommended the diving course to me.

  B It had ups and downs but he felt the second day made it worthwhile.

  C He thought it was over-priced for the amount of training he got.

  D It was something he was pleased to have tried just once.

Questions 16–20

Five sentences have been removed from the text below.

For each question, choose the correct answer.

There are three extra sentences which you do not need to use.

A fantastic opportunity

I was working as a photographer in my home town and at the time I was quite happy with my job and my life. Most of my work involved attending events like weddings, taking baby photos and normal things like that. **16** The best part of the job was meeting different types of people and feeling that my photographs made them happy.

I worked for myself so I was able to take time off whenever I wanted. **17** For that reason, I often went on several short holidays during the year, travelling to different countries. I did this for two reasons. One was the experience I was able to have of very different cultures and lifestyles. **18** I particularly enjoyed taking shots of birds and animals and I always posted these on social media when I returned home.

One day after returning from a particularly exciting trip in the mountains where I'd taken loads of pictures of wildlife, I got an unexpected phone call from a wildlife charity. They were looking for a photographer to take pictures of rare animals and they liked my pictures. They offered me the chance to travel to South Asia with their team to take photographs of snow leopards. **19** Then I thought – why not? I will only regret it if I don't!

I took up the opportunity and it was an amazing experience that I was keen to repeat. **20** What I do now is specialise in taking wildlife pictures. Sometimes it's hard because rare animals live in remote areas which can be difficult to get to, but it's so rewarding. I can't imagine ever wanting to do anything different.

A That's why I decided to say yes.

B The other was the chance to take unusual photographs.

C So after that first trip with the charity I gave up my old job.

D I enjoyed doing most of these.

E I dislike working longer hours now than I used to.

F It was nice to have that choice and it gave me freedom.

G They didn't understand my decision.

H I wasn't sure whether to accept or not.

Questions 21–26

For each question, choose the correct answer.

Water polo

Water polo is a sport which started in Scotland at the end of the nineteenth century. William Wilson, a man who was **(21)** _____ on competitive swimming, created a team game that could be played with a ball in water. He wrote down some clear **(22)** _____ and called it aquatic football, although at the time other people compared it with other sports. Some described it as **(23)** _____ to rugby but played in water. The first public game was played in the River Dee in Scotland and it became popular after that, perhaps because people didn't need much **(24)** _____ to play it.

In 1885 the Swimming Association of Great Britain **(25)** _____ on calling it water polo. People began playing it in Europe, the USA and Australia, and men's water polo was one of the first team sports introduced in the Olympic Games in 1900. However, the first women's Olympic water polo competition was not **(26)** _____ until 2000.

21	**A** pleased	**B** interested	**C** keen	**D** excited
22	**A** articles	**B** plans	**C** reports	**D** rules
23	**A** typical	**B** similar	**C** like	**D** same
24	**A** equipment	**B** property	**C** furniture	**D** material
25	**A** demanded	**B** ordered	**C** discussed	**D** insisted
26	**A** kept	**B** had	**C** held	**D** placed

Questions 27–32

For each question, write the correct answer.

Write one word for each gap.

My visit to Australia

Whenever I travel somewhere new, I try to find out about the place before I go. This was important **(27)** _____ I went to Australia last year because it is such a long way away and I didn't want to waste a moment of my time there. My plane landed in Sydney and I **(28)** _____ immediately impressed by the beautiful harbour area. Of course, I also had to visit the famous Bondi Beach and try surfing – I can tell you it's harder **(29)** _____ it looks!

There are different landscapes in Australia, from deserts to mountains, and **(30)** _____ they are all interesting, I enjoyed driving along the Great Ocean Road the most. I wanted to see some real wildlife, **(31)** _____ I did see lots of kangaroos, but I only saw a koala bear in a zoo.

Australia is such a big country it's impossible to do everything in one visit so one day I want to **(32)** _____ back!

You must answer this question.

Write your answer in about 100 words.

Question 1

Read this email from your English-speaking friend Sam and the notes you have made.

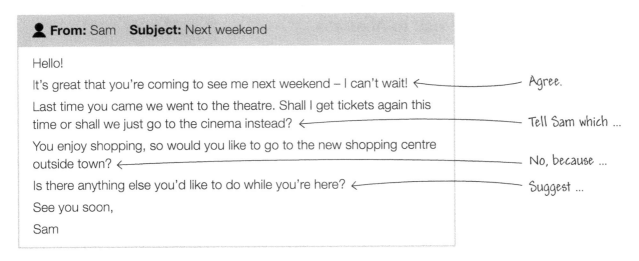

👤 **From:** Sam   **Subject:** Next weekend

Hello!

It's great that you're coming to see me next weekend – I can't wait! ← ——— Agree.

Last time you came we went to the theatre. Shall I get tickets again this time or shall we just go to the cinema instead? ← ——— Tell Sam which …

You enjoy shopping, so would you like to go to the new shopping centre outside town? ← ——— No, because …

Is there anything else you'd like to do while you're here? ← ——— Suggest …

See you soon,

Sam

Write your **email** to Sam using **all the notes**.

Choose one of these questions.

Write your answer in about 100 words.

Question 2

You see this announcement on an English-language website.

Articles wanted!

Technology!

What kind of technology do you use most? Is there any technology you don't like using so much? Why? How easy would it be to live without it?

Write an article answering these questions and we will put it on our website!

Write your **article**.

Question 3

Your English teacher has asked you to write a story.
Your story must begin with this sentence.

> *As soon as Peter met Harry in town he knew that something exciting was going to happen.*

Write your **story**.

Questions 1–7

🎧 **PE01** **For each question, choose the correct answer.**

1 What time will the bus leave for the coast?

2 Where are the friends going at the weekend?

3 What has the girl already bought for her apartment?

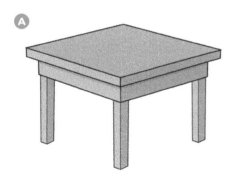  

4 Which suitcase will the boy take on holiday?

5 How much did the girl pay for her scarf?

6 Which one is the girl's cousin?

7 What date does the football competition start?

Questions 8–13

🎧 **PE02 For each question, choose the correct answer.**

8 You will hear two friends talking about a musical they saw at the theatre.
   What do they both think about it?
   A The show was funny.
   B The songs were good.
   C The singers were excellent.

9 You will hear two friends talking about a shopping website they often use.
   Why does the man like it?
   A The prices are cheap.
   B The links are easy to use.
   C The delivery service is reliable.

10 You will hear a woman telling her friend about buying concert tickets.
    What was she upset about?
    A how long it took to pay
    B how expensive they were
    C how difficult it was to choose seats

11 You will hear a man telling a friend about a trip to a different city.
    Why did he go there?
    A to see an old friend
    B to watch an event
    C to visit a museum

12 You will hear two friends talking about some changes in their sports club.
    What is the woman doing?
    A describing how people feel about them
    B explaining the reasons for them
    C complaining about their effect

13 You will hear two friends talking about a new shopping centre.
    What do they agree about it?
    A It's going to be popular.
    B The location is convenient.
    C It has a useful car park.

Questions 14–19

🎧 PE03 For each question, write the correct answer in the gap. Write one or two words or a number or a date or a time.

You will hear a woman called Ali giving a presentation about her visit to an old castle.

Ali's visit to an old historic castle

Ali was surprised about the importance of the **(14)** _____ of the castle.

Ali enjoyed listening to all the stories about **(15)** _____ the guides told visitors.

Ali's favourite part of the castle was the **(16)** _____ because of the view.

Ali was glad that there was a **(17)** _____ in part of the main building.

Ali's ticket cost **(18)** £_____ , which she didn't think was expensive.

Ali is looking forward to going to some **(19)** _____ at the castle next year.

Questions 20–25

🎧 **PE04** For each question, choose the correct answer.

You will hear an interview with a man called Jacamo Gomes, a young dancer who has just joined a professional ballet company.

20 What does Jacamo like most about dance?
    A He enjoys the music.
    B It makes him feel good.
    C It's similar to gymnastics.

21 Jacamo got the idea of becoming a dancer when
    A a teacher gave him some advice.
    B his friend took him to a particular class.
    C he identified his favourite form of dance.

22 Jacamo thinks that when training, a young dancer must
    A feel strongly about what they're doing.
    B concentrate on their movements.
    C accept help with mistakes they make.

23 How did Jacamo feel about the dance competition he took part in?
    A confident that he was the best
    B worried about the other dancers
    C surprised about the result

24 When talking about joining a professional dance company, Jacamo feels
    A excited about the new opportunities.
    B confused about how to manage his time.
    C pleased that the routine will be familiar.

25 Jacamo advises young dancers to
    A aim for perfection.
    B take every chance that comes.
    C choose which auditions to go to carefully.

PE05

Phase 1

What's your name?

Where do you live/come from?

Do you work or are you a student?

What do you do/study?

> **Extra questions**
>
> Do you have a job?
>
> Do you study?
>
> What job do you do?
>
> What subject do you study?

Phase 2

How do you travel to work or school every day? (Why?)

Did you do anything interesting yesterday? (Why? / Why not?)

Which day of the week do you like best? (Why?)

Do you prefer watching films at home or at the cinema? (Why?)

What do you enjoy doing with friends? (Why?)

Do you enjoy cooking? (Why? / Why not?)

Tell us something about your best friend.

Do you have any hobbies you really enjoy? (Why do/don't you enjoy it/them?)

> **Extra questions**
>
> Do you go to work/school by bus?
>
> What did you do yesterday?
>
> Is Monday your favourite day of the week?
>
> Do you enjoy going to the cinema?
>
> Do you go shopping with your friends?
>
> Can you cook?
>
> Who is your best friend?
>
> What do you do in your free time?

PE06

Candidate A

Now I'd like each of you to talk on your own about something.

I'm going to give each of you a photograph and I'd like you to talk about it.

Candidate A, here is your photograph. It shows people **spending an afternoon together in the countryside**.

Please tell us what you can see in the photograph.

⏱ **about 1 min.**

Extra prompts

Talk about the people.

Talk about the place.

Talk about other things in the photograph.

Candidate B

Candidate B, here is your photograph. It shows **people studying**.

Please tell us what you can see in the photograph.

⏱ **about 1 min.**

> **Extra prompts**
>
> Talk about the people.
>
> Talk about the place.
>
> Talk about other things in the photograph.

EXAM TASK

⏱ **2-3 min.**

 PE07

Now, in this part of the test you're going to talk about something together for about two minutes. I'm going to describe a situation to you.

A tennis club wants to do something special to celebrate its tenth anniversary. Here are some things the club could do to celebrate the anniversary.

Talk together about the different things the club could do to celebrate the anniversary, and say which would be most fun for all the members.

PE08

Are there many sports clubs where you live? (Why? / Why not?)

Have you ever belonged to any kind of sports club or gym? (Why? / Why not?)

What's your favourite sport? (Why?)

Do you prefer watching sport or playing it? (Why?)

Is it important for everyone to do sport? (Why? / Why not?)

Extra questions

How about you?

Do you agree?

What do you think?

LISTENING
Part 1
Practice task | Ex 1
 L01

1 Which sound does the woman prefer?

M: That programme about how different sounds make people feel was interesting.

F: Yes, it made me think! I like lots of different things. The sound of waves on a beach is relaxing – I feel quite calm when I hear that. But when my sister had a baby I loved hearing him laugh – I felt so happy. They mentioned birds singing in the programme and that can be lovely, though not my personal favourite. I always like anything connected with my family best!

2 What does the man decide to do with his friends?

F: What are you going to do with your friends this afternoon?

M: I'm not sure – they've left the decision to me. I know that some of them want to go shopping, but the town will be so busy. The weather looks nice, so I guess going out for a cycle ride is the best plan – and we haven't done that for ages, so it'll be fun. It isn't great sitting inside playing computer games when the weather's good, even though that's usually my choice.

3 What will the woman buy for her sister's wedding?

F: My sister's getting married soon and I want to buy her something nice.

M: Have you got any ideas?

F: I thought about some mugs, but she's already got lots of those. My brother's buying them a really nice kettle – it's very modern! I wish I'd thought of that. I could get a pretty vase, but it's not very exciting, and my grandmother is probably getting that. I think I'll go with my first idea – after all, you can never have too many of them!

M: It's your choice.

4 What time does the show start?

Hi, Clarrie – just to let you know that I'm going to be late tonight – I wanted to leave the office at 5 but something's come up and I can't leave until 6. There's a café opposite the theatre that's open until 6:30, so you can get something to eat before the show. If I'm not there by 7, don't wait for me, I'll meet you inside the theatre. I'll have plenty of time to get there before the curtain goes up at 7:30 so I won't miss anything.

Strategies and skills:
Predicting what you will hear | Ex 2
 L02

1 Which jacket did the man buy?

F: Did you buy a new jacket?

M: I did, and I'm pleased with it because it's very smart. My old one only had one pocket and I didn't like that – I always thought it looked rather strange. I went to lots of shops but then I saw a really nice one online which had two pockets, but I wasn't sure. My sister saw one in a local shop which was a good price and the right size, but it didn't have any pockets. So, in the end, I bought the one I found on the website.

2 How much did the woman pay for the theatre tickets?

F: Hi Agnes – just to let you know that I've got the tickets for the theatre on Friday. I didn't have a lot of choice, unfortunately, and there were none left in the cheap seats for £30. The ones for £50 were very high up and I know that you're scared of heights, so I decided to go for the most expensive tickets – I hope that £75 is OK for you. You can pay me when we meet on Friday.

3 Which sport is the man's favourite?

F: You really love sport, don't you?

M: Definitely, though the one I like best has changed. I used to play football when I was at college but I'm not so keen on it now – it's too dangerous! I tried hockey but I didn't enjoy being part of that team so now I prefer to play an individual sport. The tennis club I go to is very friendly so I prefer that to anything else.

Strategies and skills:
Predicting what you will hear | Ex 4
 L03

1 Which book is the man's favourite?

M: I love reading, and I'll try anything once! I was given a book about life in the nineteenth century for my birthday, although it wasn't really very interesting. I enjoyed a book my friend recommended about space very much – in fact, it was the best thing I'd read for ages! My sister reads anything about sport but that's not really my thing.

2 What did the woman do on her birthday?

F: I wanted to go out to a restaurant because it was my birthday but my family preferred us all to stay at home and play a boardgame. Although I was a bit annoyed at first it was OK because in the end some friends came round as a surprise and we had a good time chatting together instead. Although it wasn't exciting, it was lovely to do that as I'm usually too busy!

Strategies and skills:
Understanding distraction | Ex 8
 L04

See page 55.

EXAM TASK
 L05

1 How will the family travel to the coast?

F: Where are you going on your next holiday?

M: We're going to the coast again. It's going to be great this year. Last year we went there by car but there was so much traffic that it took ages and the parking was terrible when we got there. Because of that we did all our sightseeing by local bus. So this time we're going by train, which is quicker and better for the environment. It'll be more fun and we can rent a car if necessary.

2 What does the woman decide to do at the weekend?

M: What are you going to do this weekend?

F: Good question! I played tennis last Saturday but the weather's not looking so good this weekend.

M: No, it might rain.

F: That's right, so maybe doing something indoors is a better idea. There's the new indoor pool in town that's only just opened which could be interesting so I'll probably try that. I know my sister's going to the gym, though running on machines definitely isn't my favourite way of spending my free time!

3 What will the weather be like tomorrow?

Unfortunately, the weather's showing no signs of great improvement in the next few days, although there will be some changes. The windy conditions that covered the country yesterday will get better, although this will mean that there'll be more rain coming in from the west. The next 24 hours will be very wet indeed everywhere! Fortunately, though, temperatures will be a little warmer during the day, so we shouldn't see any snow.

4 What did the woman see on her holiday?

M: Did you see any wildlife when you were on holiday?

F: Lots! We went out on a boat and the best bit was the dolphins that swam really near us! I took loads of pictures. My friend saw some huge birds in the distance on some rocks but I missed them. Last year we went on a kind of safari because I really wanted to see some lions but, although we saw lots of other animals, they were nowhere to be seen. I'll have to try again another year!

5 Where will the man go first?

F: What are you going to do today?

M: Well, I've got different things on my list. One thing is to go to the station to collect the train tickets I bought last night online – I couldn't print them out at home.

F: If you're going that way, then could you buy some oranges? And some milk?

M: No problem! The station's near the supermarket so I guess I'll get the tickets then do the shopping. And that reminds me I need petrol, too, though I'll probably get that tomorrow.

6 How much was the woman's winter coat?

M: Did you get a new winter coat?

F: I did – I'll show you. I got a good deal, too.

M: How was that?

F: Well, I'd planned to spend around £70 and there was one I liked online for £60. I nearly bought it but I decided to go and look in that big department store first – my friend said there were special discounts there this week. The coat I got was reduced twice – from £85 to £60 and finally to £50! You should look yourself tomorrow – there are men's coats for around £85.

7 Which musical instrument does the man enjoy playing most?

F: You're busy these days – are you still taking lots of music lessons?

M: I am! The problem is having enough time to do them all because I don't want to give any of them up. I thought the guitar would be my favourite as I can play it with friends, but actually I prefer the sound of the piano. It's rather lonely playing it on my own, though. The violin's turned out to be my top choice because I can play it in an orchestra. That makes me try harder to improve!

LISTENING
Part 2
Practice task | Ex 1
🎧 L06
See page 58.

Strategies and skills:
Identifying a speaker's attitude | Ex 3
🎧 L07

1 What does the man think about his holiday?

F: How was the holiday?

M: Well, we did a lot of nice things, like cycling, and the food in the hotel was great. In the end, though, it wasn't as good as I'd expected it to be because everything was quite expensive and the weather was poor.

2 What does the woman think about the film?

M: I loved that film!

F: I quite enjoyed it on the whole, although the soundtrack was really annoying me – it was so loud! The actors did an amazing job, though, and I believed in all of their characters. I guess it was worth seeing.

3 What does the man think about his birthday party?

F: How was your birthday party?

M: Good question! I didn't think anyone would arrange a big birthday party for me unexpectedly and so when I got home from work and all my friends were there I couldn't believe it. In a way that spoiled it, because I found it difficult to relax completely – I like to be able to look forward to something!

4 What does the woman think about her college course?

M: What do you think about your course?

F: It's going really well, even though it's difficult for me to go to everything because I have to work in the evenings and that's when some of the lectures take place. I'm still learning a lot though and I'm glad I'm doing it.

5 What does the man think about buying expensive clothes?

F: That's a nice coat!

M: Thanks! I paid more for it than usual but I'm very pleased. I know some people won't do that because they don't think it's worth it but I think if you buy good quality, you enjoy it more and it makes a better impression on other people.

6 What does the woman think about her new job?

M: Are you enjoying your new job?

F: Well, there are lots of good things about it. The office is nearer to home so getting there is much easier, and the hours are better for me. Unfortunately, I'm still learning what I need to do and I'm often not sure about things. I guess it'll just take me time to get used to it!

Strategies and skills:
Listening for agreement or disagreement | Ex 5

 L08

1

M: A lot of people think that failure is a bad thing but actually it can make us try harder. I think it's sometimes more useful than doing well, and it's all part of learning.

F: It's quite hard to deal with emotionally, though. It makes me feel I'm not good enough.

2

F: I like it when my teacher tells me what I've done wrong. I can learn from my mistakes then.

M: It helps you to see what isn't right and that's really helpful.

3

M: I find it difficult to give a good impression when I meet someone for the first time because I get embarrassed very easily.

F: You just have to feel confident and believe in yourself – it's really not that hard.

4

F: Job interviews are very stressful because it's important to look good.

M: There's certainly a lot of pressure, especially if you really want to get the job.

5

M: It's important to smile when you meet someone for the first time.

F: You also have to speak nicely, though – in fact what you say is more important.

6

F: I really notice other people's body language – it's important to get it right.

M: It's actually one of the things that can cause misunderstandings, so we need to be aware of it.

7

M: I like having lots of friends – it's good to have people to talk to if I have problems.

F: I'm not sure that it's possible to have a lot of <u>real</u> friends – I prefer to have just one or two that I really trust.

8

F: That film was thrilling – I couldn't take my eyes off the screen.

M: I couldn't always concentrate because I wasn't really interested in the characters.

1 You will hear two friends talking about a film they have just seen.

M: That was so disappointing. I expected it to be amazing as the people in it are such big stars.

F: Yes, and actually I thought their performances were the best part of it.

M: Really? I've seen them do better. But did you understand what was going on? I was completely lost most of the time.

F: It was pretty difficult to follow. I guess that's because it was science fiction, so it was a bit odd.

M: But that's another thing – those scenes on other planets were so dull and not really creative.

F: Oh, I didn't really notice.

2 You will hear a woman telling a friend about a bus journey she made.

M: I saw you were late this morning. Did you have a problem on the road?

F: I missed the first bus, even though the bus stop's near my house, so I don't have far to walk to catch it. The journey was quicker than I expected, but it was so boring!

M: Don't you usually drive?

F: Definitely, but my car's in the garage this week so I had no choice. I think that tomorrow I'll see if a neighbour can give me a lift.

3 You will hear a man telling a friend about his holiday.

F: Did you have a good holiday?

M: It was great! I went with a group of friends and there was loads of stuff we could do together – sailing, water skiing, diving – we tried them all and I've never had such fun. The weather was fantastic, which made a big difference.

F: How about the accommodation?

M: It was a good standard and right on the beach – the only thing was how far it was from the town. We had to get taxis if we wanted to go out in the evening. I'd go there again, though.

4 You will hear two friends talking about buying music.

M: Do you ever buy CDs these days?

F: Very rarely. Maybe when there's a special version of something that I want to keep. I download everything. I spend ages doing it though, especially if there's a connection problem and it keeps stopping. The thing is, it's cheaper. There's more variety of music I like online, too. Plus I don't have to buy a whole load of songs by just one singer like you do on a CD – that just wastes money.

M: I agree – I don't know anyone who doesn't download music – all my music's on my phone.

5 You will hear two friends talking about a new computer game.

F: Are you still playing that new game?

M: Yes! I couldn't stop until I got to the next level. I was really enjoying the story.

F: Last night I couldn't get into it properly, so I took a break and did other stuff I like just as much. Then I went back and played a bit more. I didn't realise how late it was when I stopped!

M: I know what you mean! You're thinking about so many things when you're playing.

F: At least it's not stressful, so it didn't stop me sleeping like some games do. I'll carry on with it tonight.

6 You will hear a woman telling a friend about a coat she has just bought.

M: Is that a new coat?

F: Yes, I only bought it last week. It took me ages to decide to get it but it was such a lovely blue that I had to have it. The only thing now is that I saw one in a different shop yesterday that I like just as much, so I'm confused.

M: I think it looks nice.

F: Thanks. It's normally quite a bit more than I'd want to pay but it was on special offer and so I got a good discount. I guess I'll keep it now.

LISTENING
Part 3
Practice task | Ex 1 and Ex 7

 L10 and L11

See page 64.

Strategies and skills:
Listening for figures | Ex 1

 L12

1   The concert will be on the 14th of November.
2   I was born in 1990.
3   The lesson will be later today and won't start until 6:50.
4   The train leaves at 7:12.
5   The book costs £5.05.
6   I drove 2,030 miles on my holiday and now I'm back home I'm exhausted!

Strategies and skills:
Listening for figures | Ex 2

 L13

1
M: When's your birthday, Chloe? Mine's the 15th of September.
F: It's on the 4th of November, so I'm younger than you.
2
M: When were you born, Gemma? I was born in 2002.
F: In 1999.
3
M: What time's the train leaving, Sara? I can't get there until 6:10.
F: Not sure – I think it's 6:15 from platform 7.

4
F: Any idea what time the film starts, Adam? Ali said it was seven o'clock.
M: Well, the programme starts at 7 but there are advertisements first so it's probably not before 7:20.
5
M: How much was the book, Jac? It looks expensive!
F: I think it was £6.50 originally but I got a discount so it cost me £5.95.
6
F: How many people are coming to the conference, Luke?
M: Last year it was 200, so I expect it'll be around 230 this time.

Strategies and skills:
Listening for spelling | Ex 3

 L14

1   w-e-a-r
2   w-e-a-t-h-e-r
3   t-h-e-r-e
4   b-a-c-k
5   a-l-i-v-e
6   s-i-t

Strategies and skills:
Listening for spelling | Ex 4

 L15

1   The website address is www.delartang.com – that's d-e-l-a-r-t-a-n-g.com.
2   Please email Janicewethur@history.com – that's j-a-n-i-c-e-w-e-t-h-u-r @history.com.
3   The school is called Laykord Academy – that's L-a-y-k-o-r-d Academy.
4   The address you want is 24, Alwornter Street – that's a-l-w-o-r-n-t-e-r Street.
5   You should contact Peter Hisporcutt – that's h-i-s-p-o-r-c-u-t-t.
6   The town is in the north and it's called Birchering, that's b-i-r-c-h-e-r-i-n-g.

Strategies and skills: Identifying the kind of information you need | Ex 6

 L16

1   I really enjoy all kinds of holidays. My favourite one was in the mountains last year. We did a lot of walking but I loved it because of the skiing and that's what I like best!
2   I had turned down the chance to go to Paris with my sister and our cousin last year, which I regretted. Then I visited an art gallery in London with a friend who told me about the galleries in Paris and said I should go. So I did!
3   Hi, Gill. We need to plan when to meet this evening. The film starts at 7 so I think that 6:30 is about right – 6 would give us too much time to wait. We don't want to eat first, do we? So see you then!
4   I'm very happy with my coat – it was in a local shop for £85 but I got it online for only £65. It's the first time I've done that but it won't be the last!

5 The museum shop was really good. I bought myself a silk scarf, which is lovely, and a book for my sister. She loves history so I know she'll like it.

6 I liked the science museum very much, especially the model spaceship. The guide said that the old train was the thing most visitors preferred, though, and that surprised me.

7 For anyone doing the tour of the theatre this afternoon, please go to reception to meet your guide. The tour itself begins at the stage door at 2:30.

8 When I decided to take part in the race, I thought that it would only be a few people – ten at most. I was so surprised when I got to the start and there were 50! Obviously I didn't win!

Strategies and skills:
Identifying incorrect answers | Ex 7

 L17

See page 66.

Strategies and skills:
Identifying incorrect answers | Ex 9

 L18

See page 66.

Strategies and skills:
Checking grammar | Ex 11

 L19

1 Please remember that you must bring proper walking boots, but I guess you all know that. What you may not realise is that it's useful to have a towel in case it rains while we're out in the hills.

2 The friends had a great day out and the best part was swimming in the sea. It was a great beach to go to!

3 I love cooking and that means I love eating, too! The food I like best is fruit, especially apples, although I do like oranges as well.

4 Hockey is my favourite sport and I play as a goalkeeper. It can be dangerous so it's necessary to put on a helmet during a match. Of course, you have to carry your stick as well!

5 When I decided to go on holiday to the island, I knew that it rained a lot so I expected to get wet. Luckily, the five days I was there it was dry, which was lovely!

6 Lucy's artwork is wonderful and she puts her best work on the website. I want her to put some in the college magazine as well one day.

EXAM TASK

 L20

Examiner: You will hear a woman called Alina giving a presentation about a chocolate-making course she went on.

F: Hi, everyone! I'm Alina and I'm here to talk about a course I did recently. I wanted to do some kind of cookery course but I wasn't sure which one. All the courses took place in different local restaurants. I found some information on Bake Restaurant but that course was about bread. I thought about making fish dishes in Fry Restaurant but in the end I chose the one in Sweet Restaurant because it was about chocolate.

The course was two days long. There were shorter courses in the evenings which were cheaper – only £30 for two hours – but I wanted to do more than learn the basics. Mine cost £150 but that was with a discount as I booked in advance. There were nine other people on my course and they paid £175.

The classes took place in a special kitchen above the restaurant. On the first morning the instructors told us about the history of chocolate and let us taste and identify flavours in different desserts. The most popular was strawberry but I loved coconut. I wasn't keen on pear, which didn't taste so strong.

We all had slightly different interests. Most people wanted to make chocolate cakes or biscuits but I thought sweets would be more fun. On the second day we could choose what we made so I did that.

I didn't realise how difficult chocolate is to work with. You have to be very careful to keep it at the right temperature and not let it get too hot or too cold. It can sometimes change colour, too, though that's less important. It took me ages to get it right!

I really enjoyed the experience and since then I've heard of other more advanced courses. If any of you are interested, there's information about all the courses in this area on the website at www.chokyum.com – that's c-h-o-k-y-u-m. I really recommend it!

LISTENING

Part 4

Practice task | Ex 1

 L21

See page 68.

Strategies and skills:
Listening for opinions | Ex 2

 L22

1

M: I don't know how I'd live without my mobile phone – I use it all the time.

F: Well, I think we all use our phones too much. We ought to turn them off for at least an hour every day – then we could see if we can manage without them for a while.

M: Sorry – that's impossible! I couldn't do it.

2

F: I recycle everything I can but that's all I do. It's enough, really.

M: I don't agree with that. I don't think people are aware of the problems of the environment and there should be more information about it. Recycling is only a small part of it.

3

M: The first thing I do when I get home is put on some music.

F: Definitely. Listening to it on my phone isn't as good and it's sometimes hard to hear it when I'm travelling to work. That's quite stressful, so it's better to read a book.

M: I don't find that at all – I think music is always relaxing wherever I listen to it! It's a great way to pass the time on a long journey.

4

F: I enjoy my job – it's interesting and I don't mind working long hours.

M: I made the decision not to work too much – I want to have time to spend with my family and take up new hobbies.

F: I know what you mean – I definitely can't do that.

5

M: Did you see those photos in the press when he was on holiday? I don't think that's right.

F: No – it must be very difficult when that happens. On the other hand, he has a great life with lots of money so it's not that bad. I could live with it!

M: I think it's more difficult than you imagine.

6

F: I love reading the things people put on social media – they seem to have such interesting lives!

M: Do you really think it's true? I don't think it is – people are trying to show that they have interesting lives but it's usually not real.

F: Well, I like to think that it is!

Strategies and skills:
Identifying reasons | Ex 3

 L23

1 Everyone should play a musical instrument because it makes people feel happy.

2 We all know a lot more about wildlife due to television documentaries.

3 My interests include bird-watching and wildlife photography so I choose to live in the countryside.

4 I'd love to sing on stage but the problem is that I have a terrible voice!

5 The new film had great reviews and that's why I'm going to see it on Saturday.

6 I stayed up late last night and that's the reason why I'm tired today.

7 I joined a gym so that I could get fit.

8 I usually study at the weekends in order to get a good grade at college.

Strategies and skills:
Identifying the main idea | Ex 4

 L24

1 I tend to buy clothes quickly – I don't waste time in the shop seeing if they fit me – that's boring, and I'm good at knowing my size. I always choose things that are on offer or a good price. Does that mean I make bad decisions? Sometimes, because clothes may be cheap for a reason! I don't think I'll change, though.

2 People buy too many things. I don't know whether that's because we enjoy shopping more than we used to or whether we just throw things away too easily. It's a fact that we buy new things and throw old things away without thinking about it very much, and that's not good. When I was younger I used to save money to buy something and then I kept it for a long time. Maybe that was better.

3 One of the most popular leisure activities nowadays is shopping and people love it. But the result is that our homes become full of stuff we've bought without thinking and probably don't need. Once that happens it's difficult to know what to do with them and it's not easy to decide what to throw away.

4 It's interesting that unlike their parents, many young people often choose to own as little as possible – a phone seems to be enough! This could be because they don't have much money but that's probably not true. They want to spend their money on enjoying themselves, not on buying things.

5 We're surrounded by advertisements. They appear on every website we visit and it's very hard to ignore them. So we should teach children to look at them carefully and not to buy something just because the advertisement they see on television is fun. That's an important life skill.

6 Normally I hate any kind of shopping but I love buying presents for friends and family. I enjoy thinking about what to choose and whether they will like it. That's much more enjoyable than buying something for myself because then I think walking round the shops is such a waste of time!

7 I do buy things online. Prices are often lower, which is a good thing, but I can't be sure that the pictures of what I'm buying are real. I've often had to send things back, which costs money. If I go to the shops in town, I can meet my friends and we can have a nice time together. That's much more fun so price doesn't matter!

8 Shopping's become a social activity for my friends but I hate it. The shops are busy, it's difficult to park, walking round is tiring – it's definitely not relaxing. I worry about spending too much money and I don't think I'm alone. I don't know why some people do it so often!

Strategies and skills:
Recognising distractors | Ex 6

 L25

See page 70.

Strategies and skills:
Recognising distractors | Ex 8

 L26

It would be easy for me to go crazy and write about all kinds of strange food. Unfortunately, that wouldn't be popular with people who don't want to spend a lot of time and effort in their kitchens at home. So I have to use normal ingredients that you can find everywhere and make my recipes clear and not difficult to follow. I want to share my love of food but not make things impossible for people to cook!

Strategies and skills:
Recognising distractors | Ex 10

 L27

Every day I think up ideas, note them down and then my team of cooks try to follow them to make the dish. They cook everything I've planned several times, just to make sure that my instructions actually work. It's a great feeling when everything goes well! I don't particularly like the final writing part or taking photos to go in the book – that's someone else's job.

EXAM TASK

 L28

M: Today I'm speaking to Carrie Silver, a young writer who is famous for her poetry. Carrie, why is poetry special for you?

F: As a child I loved listening to my mum reading aloud. There's something about language that appeals to me – I hear words almost like music. Then when I began writing my own stuff I started by playing with that and I think that's at the heart of my poetry. I don't focus on what I want to say but how people will hear it.

M: Why did you decide to make poetry your career?

F: I'm shy and not very good at talking to people but poetry gave me a voice. I just wanted to write and didn't really think about whether I could get rich from it. Maybe it's something to do with having to choose words carefully but I felt as though I was maybe better than most other people at that.

M: How do you feel when you're writing poetry?

F: I've become less nervous, though I do show ideas to friends whose opinion I value. Sometimes I change things and it's obviously important to listen to other people but in the end it's my poem and I trust myself. I've also learnt to wait before making any decisions – looking at something again is useful.

M: Tell us more about the way you write poetry.

F: I can get an idea anywhere but then I keep it in my head for a while. I let it grow and develop without working with it and it takes on a life of its own. That's very creative but it can be a bit stressful. Then I note down actual words and think about how long the poem will be – that can be hard work. But it's typing the finished thing on the computer that makes it real and gives me the biggest thrill.

M: Now you're writing a play. That must be very different from poetry!

F: It's challenging! In poetry you know what your message is and you've planned it but in a play you have to produce a narrative that actors can bring their own ideas to. That was difficult at first but now I love hearing other people's thoughts. It's exciting to let someone else bring my words to life, although the whole process takes much longer than I'd like. And of course nothing's perfect – I always see things I want to change later on but by then it's too late.

M: Do you have any advice for young writers?

F: Find writers you love and think about what it is you like about them. Once you've identified what that is, you'll have something to aim for. But don't just write about the same things because you need to make your work different from theirs. You have to be original if you want to be a success!

SPEAKING
Part 1
Practice task | Ex 1 and Ex 6

 S01 and S04

See page 72.

Practice task | Ex 3 and Ex 5

 S02 and S03

1

Examiner: What's your name?

A: My name is Caroline but my friends call me Caro.

2

Examiner: Where do you come from?

A: Paris, which is in northern France.

3

Examiner: Do you work or are you a student?

A: I'm a student.

4

Examiner: What do you do or study?

A: I study English at college.

5

Examiner: What do you like doing in your free time?

A: I like playing any sport, especially tennis.

6

Examiner: What did you do yesterday?

A: I went to the cinema yesterday and watched a film about the future.

7

Examiner: Is there a city you would like to visit in the future?

A: I think I would like to visit New York.

8

Examiner: Do you use social media very often?

A: It depends, but usually every day.

Strategies and skills:
Answering questions | Ex 2

 S05

1

Examiner: Where do you live?

F: In Genoa, in Italy.

2

Examiner: What do you usually do in the evenings?

M: I usually chat to my friends online.

3

Examiner: What's your favourite sport?

F: Definitely football because I love team sports.

4

Examiner: How often do you look at your mobile phone?

F: Probably every ten minutes or so!

5

Examiner: What did you do last weekend?

M: I went to the beach with my family.

6

Examiner: Who is your best friend?

F: Julia – I've known her for years as she lives next door to me.

EXAM TASK

 S06

See page 74.

Example answer

 S07

Examiner: What's your name?

F: My name is Sue, although my family call me Susie.

Examiner: Where do you live or come from?

F: I live in Amsterdam now but I come from France.

Examiner: Do you work or are you a student?

F: I work in a school.

Examiner: What do you do or study?

F: I teach French to Dutch students.

Examiner: What do you have for breakfast every day?

F: It depends. I usually have toast but I always have coffee!

Examiner: What did you do last weekend?

F: I went to a museum to see a special exhibition. It was very interesting.

Examiner: What job would you like to do in the future?

F: I like my job at the moment but in the future I would like to work in a lot of different countries.

Examiner: Tell us about your favourite sport.

F: Oh that's easy – it's basketball. I play it every weekend and I think I'm quite good.

SPEAKING

Part 2

Practice task | Ex 1

 S08

See page 75.

Practice task | Ex 2

 S09

A: OK – er – it's a house – it's a kitchen in a house or flat and it's daytime. There are two people in the kitchen – a man and a boy – and they're cooking something to eat. The man has a … er … pan … er … and the boy has a knife. He's cutting things … vegetables … er … maybe peppers … and he looks happy. The man looks happy, too. They're enjoying themselves. The boy is wearing a shirt and jeans. The man is wearing a shirt and he has a … er … beard.

B: I can see two people who are cooking something and I think they're at home in their kitchen. It's a modern kitchen and the house looks nice. The people cooking are a father and his small son. The father is cooking something using a frying pan and he is looking at what the boy is doing. He is cutting up vegetables for his father to cook – I can see carrots, peppers and other things – but I don't know what they're called.
The boy is wearing a striped T-shirt and jeans and he's sitting on a high chair because he's too small to reach the table. His father is wearing a blue shirt and white T-shirt. They both look happy and I think they are enjoying themselves.

Practice task | Ex 6

 S10

I can see a family eating a meal at home. They're sitting around a table in their kitchen and eating and talking. On the right there's a boy wearing a checked shirt and he's sitting next to his mother who is smiling at him. On the left-hand side there's a girl with long hair – I think she's his sister – and she's wearing a striped top. In the middle of the picture is their father, who's wearing a blue shirt. They're eating a big meal, including bread, which is in the middle of the table, and some kind of salad. They're drinking water with their meal. Behind them I can see some kitchen cupboards and a potted plant. It's a very modern kitchen which is very tidy.

Strategies and skills:
Speaking fluently | Ex 7 and Ex 8

 S11 and S12

The photograph shows people sightseeing in a city. In the background I can see the city and it's very modern and there are lots of tall buildings. In the middle of the picture there's a river or a lake – I'm not sure. The people are all standing on a … I can't remember the word, maybe it's a platform, and they're obviously tourists. I think they're enjoying the amazing view. They're all wearing casual clothes, for example the man on the right is wearing a white T-shirt and jeans. The woman in the middle is wearing a yellow jacket and she's also carrying a bag. Some people are taking photographs of the city. I think one man has a kind of camera but one girl is using her mobile phone instead. So what else can I say – the weather is lovely and the sky is blue.

Strategies and skills:
Linking ideas | Ex 10

 S13

I can see two friends studying together. They're sitting outside on the grass and they're working together – perhaps they're doing their homework or helping each other to finish a project. The man on the right is wearing a checked shirt and brown trousers and he's showing his friend something he's written in a notebook. They're both smiling about it. The man on the left is wearing a yellow sweatshirt, blue jeans and striped trainers. He has headphones round his neck so I guess he's listening to music while he's working. There's also a laptop open in front of him so he's probably using that to do his work. Behind the two friends I can see a building which may be their college.

Strategies and skills:
What to describe/giving a description | Ex 15

 S14

So the people are in a park because there are trees, and fences along the path and there are other people in the background. There are three women and they all look happy – they're cycling together and talking at the same time. They are all wearing casual clothes and it doesn't look cold – I think it is sunny. The woman on the right is wearing a blue shirt and a scarf and she has short hair. The woman in the middle has long hair and she's wearing a black jacket. The woman on the left is wearing a shirt, erm … a spotted shirt, and she's wearing blue shoes. Behind them I can see a … just a minute … a wooden house, but I don't know what it is, and there's a lamppost on the right.

Strategies and skills:
What to describe/giving a description | Ex 16

 S15

See page 80.

EXAM TASK

 S16

See page 81.

Example answer

 S17

Examiner: Now I'd like each of you to talk on your own about something. I'm going to give each of you a photograph and I'd like you to talk about it.

Candidate A, here is your photograph. It shows people having a music lesson. Please tell us what you can see in the photograph.

A: So in my photograph I can see people having a music lesson – it's a man and a woman who are learning to play the guitar. They look interested and seem to be concentrating. Their teacher is on the left of the photograph and he's helping the girl. He's wearing a red sweater. The two students are sitting on a sofa in the middle of the photograph, and behind them there are shelves with lots of things on – I'm not sure what they are. The girl has long hair and she's wearing a sweater and trousers. The other student has long hair, too, and he's wearing a striped sweater and trousers. In front of them there's a table with papers on it and a lamp and a laptop. So what else can I say? The room's a bit untidy!

Examiner: Candidate B, here is your photograph. It shows people waiting to travel at an airport. Please tell us what you can see in the photograph.

B: I can see a group of people waiting at an airport. The airport looks very modern with very big windows. I can see planes outside. I think all the people are friends and they're probably going on holiday because they have bags with them. They're all sitting on the floor and looking at their mobile phones while they're waiting for their plane. They're wearing casual clothes and trainers. The man in the middle of the group is wearing a dark T-shirt and he has a small blue bag in front of him. The man on his left is wearing a kind of shirt but it's white, and he has a pair of sunglasses and a bigger black bag – it looks like a rucksack. The girl on the left of the photograph is wearing a blue T-shirt and the girl on the right has a big blue bag on her shoulder. She has long hair. They all look relaxed.

SPEAKING

Part 3

Practice task | Ex 1

 S18
See page 82.

Practice task | Ex 3, Ex 4, Ex 5 and Ex 6

S19, S20, S21 and S22

M: So we have to talk about what new sport this young man can do to keep fit. Do you think rock climbing's a good idea?

F: He doesn't have much time to learn a new sport and rock climbing's very difficult. I don't think that's a good idea. What about cycling? That's easy and it doesn't take long to learn. Everyone can cycle!

M: Well, I don't like it much – it's quite uncomfortable! It's probably a good way to keep fit, though, and better than rock climbing.

F: What do you think about swimming? It's a fun way to keep fit.

M: I agree with you about that. It's easy to learn, too, and there are lots of courses at swimming pools to improve your technique.

F: Do you like yoga? I haven't done it but it's probably a good idea.

M: I don't agree because I think it looks very boring.
I prefer to do something a bit more exciting – have a bit of competition.

F: Do you mean like tennis? But you need someone to play with and he doesn't have much time. That could be difficult to organise.

M: Yes, that's a problem. OK – let's choose running because he can do that whenever he wants on his own and there's not much to learn.

F: That's a good choice.

Strategies and skills: Making suggestions and recommendations | Ex 3

 S23

M: So, we have to make suggestions for this young woman in the city. What do you think?

F: I think she should join a club, something like a music club. That's a great way to meet people – much better than using social media.

M: True, but she may not like music. How about talking to neighbours? She can always go and see them in the evenings and she won't be lonely.

F: But neighbours may not always be at home. I think she ought to take up a sport. It's healthy and fun. That's more useful than going to museums.

M: OK, I agree.

Strategies and skills: Agreeing and disagreeing | Ex 6

 S24

1

M: I think that everyone should do some kind of exercise – we should try to keep fit.

F: I think the same but it's not always easy.

2

F: I think it's nice to have a short break occasionally – I enjoy going away for the weekend.

M: That's a good point, though it's quite expensive if you stay in a hotel.

3

M: People use mobile phones too much nowadays – it's not good.

F: I'm not sure about that. I couldn't manage without mine!

4

F: I really enjoy shopping – it's a great way to spend a Saturday afternoon!

M: That's not what I think. It's so boring!

5

M: It's a good idea to live in different countries if you can – you learn so much.

F: I'm sure you're right. It's a great experience.

6

F: In my opinion, everyone should learn to cook.

M: Sorry, I don't think so. I'd rather have a takeaway!

EXAM TASK

 S25

See page 85.

Example answer

 S26

Examiner: Now, in this part of the test you're going to talk about something together for about two minutes. I'm going to describe a situation to you.

A young man wants to give his parents a present for their 25th wedding anniversary. He doesn't have much money to spend but he wants his parents to feel special.

Here are some things he could give his parents.

Talk together about the things he could give his parents, and say which would be best.

M: So we have to talk about the presents he can give his parents for their anniversary. What do you think about the theatre tickets?

F: Well, he should give them something special but they'll be expensive because he'll have to buy them good seats. That's why I'm not sure they're a good idea. He could give them a framed photograph of the whole family – they'd like that.

M: But they've probably got lots of photographs like that! What do you think about the flowers? People always like those.

F: Yes, that's right, but then they're not very special, are they? How about the camera? They can keep that for a long time and it's always nice to have lots of pictures to look at when they're on their own.

M: That's true, though I just use my mobile phone for taking photos. I don't know whether they use their phones, too, and a good camera will be expensive. The books are a nice idea if they like cooking, and they might not cost a lot. I definitely don't think he should give them a cake.

F: I agree! Oh, look, we haven't talked about the vase. That could be a good suggestion because they can keep it and when they look at it they'll remember their anniversary. I think we should choose that – do you agree?

M: That's a good point about remembering the anniversary. OK – I agree – let's go with your idea.

SPEAKING

Part 4

Practice task | Ex 1

 S27

See page 86.

SPEAKING

Part 4

Practice task | Ex 2, Ex 3, Ex 4 and Ex 7

 **S28, S29, S30 and S31**

1

Examiner: Do you usually buy presents for friends when you go on holiday?

M: I sometimes buy a small present for a friend when I go on holiday so that they know I was thinking of them and I can share my experience with them, too. But it's a mistake to spend a lot of holiday time looking for something they might not like and I hate shopping anyway!

2

Examiner: Do you buy many holiday souvenirs for yourself?

F: I always buy myself something so that I can remember the holiday but it's usually something useful – not just a pretty picture or something like that. My favourite souvenir is a scarf I bought in Italy – I wear it a lot and I bought it really quickly in a small shop on the beach!

3

Examiner: Is it always important to spend a lot of money on a present for someone else?

F: I'm not sure about that. I think it's nice to spend a lot of money but only if I'm sure that the person will like it. In my opinion it's a mistake to spend a lot of money on something they might not like!

Examiner: What do you think, Juan?

M: I agree with Maria. Personally, I believe that it's important to spend more money if it's a special birthday or anniversary present. It doesn't matter if it's not a special occasion.

4

Examiner: Have you ever made a present for someone instead of buying a present for them?

F: I don't do that very often but I have done it sometimes, like when I wanted to give someone a special present. For example, I made a book of photographs for my mother. Another thing I did was I painted a card for my grandmother. She liked that!

5

Examiner: Do you think it's more enjoyable to give a present to someone else or to receive one yourself?

F: I definitely prefer giving someone else a present, even if it's difficult to choose something, because I like to see how happy they are when they open it. It's more fun than getting something myself.

M: I don't agree at all. I like giving presents but I love getting a lot of presents myself, especially when it's a surprise present from a friend because it's nice to get something you're not expecting.

Strategies and skills:
Describing opinions, likes and dislikes | Ex 2

🎧 S32

F: I really enjoy my course – the teachers are great and the lessons are so interesting.

M: It seems to me that there's too much work to do in the evenings – I hate having to do that!

F: Well, I find that if I do that work quickly, I still have time to enjoy myself.

M: Maybe I just prefer enjoying myself to working, then!

EXAM TASK

🎧 S33

See page 87.

Example answer

🎧 S34

Examiner: What do you usually do when you want to relax?

F: I love reading and I think it's very relaxing to do that because I can forget myself and just enjoy the story.

Examiner: Do you think watching sport is relaxing?

M: I enjoy watching sport, especially football, but I don't think it's relaxing because I always want my team to win!

Examiner: What do you think?

F: Oh, I'm not keen on sport, although my father loves it! I prefer reading.

Examiner: Do you sometimes choose to do nothing in the evenings or do you always like to be busy?

F: I've got so much to do – studying, working and things like that – that it's difficult for me to do nothing. I have always got something to do!

Examiner: If you're on holiday, do you prefer to do lots of sightseeing or to take it easy?

M: I like to do both, for example if I'm in a city, then I love going to museums; but if I'm near the sea, then I'm keen on just doing nothing except sitting on the beach. It's important to take things easy sometimes!

Examiner: Do you agree?

F: Yes, I do. I remember a fantastic holiday one year when we went to an amazing city and spent all the time looking round but I do also like lying on the beach.

Examiner: Do you think it's important to turn off your mobile phone sometimes so that you can relax?

M: I think that's a very difficult question! I use my phone all the time – to contact my friends and to check on what's happening. I hate being without it so that's not relaxing – it's actually rather stressful!

Practice Exam

LISTENING

Part 1

🎧 PE01

1 What time will the bus leave for the coast?

Hi, everyone! I want to give you some information about the trip to the coast tomorrow. The bus will take us to a small resort where there are lots of activities, like swimming and hiking. The roads are narrow so the drive takes about 85 minutes. Please be at the bus stop outside the hotel by 8:15 at the latest so we can set off at 8:30. We're booked in for lunch at a nice local restaurant at 12:45 so you won't be hungry!

2 Where are the friends going at the weekend?

F: Hi, Peter! What shall we do this weekend?

M: I was hoping we could go swimming but my friend says the pool's closed for a week for repairs.

F: That's a shame! I suppose we could just play tennis instead – I'd like that.

M: Or we could try that new skateboarding park on the other side of town. I've heard it's very good. We could even go to the cinema afterwards.

F: My brother's got my skateboard and the weather's too good to be inside anyway.

M: So it looks like we go for your suggestion then.

3 What has the girl already bought for her apartment?

Hi, Mum! I'm calling to say there's no need to look for a small table for my new apartment. I've just seen exactly what I want at the shop in town so I've paid for it and they're delivering it on Friday. I know dad still wants to buy me something and what I'd really like is a nice mirror for the bathroom. I've asked gran to get me a lamp, and she can choose that, so then I've got everything I need. Speak soon!

4 Which suitcase will the boy take on holiday?

F: I've packed my bag for the holiday already. Have you?

M: No – I can't decide which suitcase to take. Last year I took the one with stripes, but the lock's broken. I've got two others – which one do you think is best?

F: Well, if you want my advice, the one with spots'll be easy to identify when we're travelling. You might lose the plain one or get confused about which one's yours – there are loads of cases like that.

M: Good point. I'll do what you've suggested.

5 How much did the girl pay for her scarf?

M: That's a lovely scarf you're wearing.

F: Thanks. I only bought it last month. I'd seen it online for £25, which seemed to be cheaper than in the shops, but it was still a bit expensive. I wasn't sure about the quality, either. Then a friend told me about a new shop in town that had special discounts so I looked there and it was £23 so I went ahead. I've seen special offers of £20 online since then though, which is a bit annoying!

6 Which one is the girl's cousin?

F: My cousin's coming to visit the college next Tuesday. It's a shame I won't be there on that day, 'cos I have a dentist appointment. You must say hello to him.

M: Did I meet him last year? Isn't he the one with the very short curly hair?

F: He's got straight blond hair and he's very tall. Maybe you met my brother – he's got curly hair, but it's dark.

M: Does your cousin wear glasses?

F: No, though my brother does.

M: I'll look out for him.

7 What date does the football competition start?

Before the competition begins I want to confirm some important dates with you, starting with our next training session, which will be on the 3rd of March. After that we'll carry on with normal weekly practice until the first match on the 15th of April but then we'll increase it to three sessions a week. The final game is on the 1st of May. Our most difficult one will be against Leyton. Don't worry about it, though, as I'm confident you'll win it easily after our training.

LISTENING

Part 2

 PE02

8 You will hear two friends talking about a musical they saw at the theatre.

F: I enjoyed that.

M: Me, too! I don't often go to the theatre and it's nice to see a good musical play. The quality of everyone's singing on stage was really high.

F: I wasn't sure about the main singer – I didn't like her voice so that spoilt it for me. What she was singing was great, though.

M: I hadn't heard the soundtrack before and I was really impressed. I laughed a lot, too, which I like when I go to the theatre.

F: Well, it was more serious than I expected.

9 You will hear two friends talking about a shopping website they often use.

F: I've just bought loads of stuff on that shopping website – I really like it.

M: I use it a lot, too, though I do find some parts of the site a bit confusing, like when I click on something it doesn't always take me to the right place. On the other hand, it's convenient to be able to order something and get it the next day – they've never got my order wrong and it always arrives on time. Sometimes things are more expensive than in the local shop, though, so I guess you're paying for that.

F: You're probably right.

10 You will hear a woman telling her friend about buying concert tickets.

M: Did you get tickets for the rock concert next month?

F: I did, although it wasn't easy. When I logged onto the website there were still some good lower-priced seats available, though they were rather high up and quite a long way from the stage. I managed to select them and put them into my basket but then it took ages to fill in my credit card information because the page kept disappearing. I was getting really worried that I might lose them, but I didn't. I will complain to the organisers about it, though.

M: I think you should.

11 You will hear a man telling a friend about a trip to a different city.

F: How was your trip?

M: Really good, thanks. I was even able to visit that new museum while I was there – it was interesting.

F: I've never been there, even though I know it's not far away.

M: And the football competition, which was my main reason for being there of course, was so exciting! I was glad I'd bought a ticket. Someone I used to go to school with lives in the city and I thought we might be able to meet for coffee. He was busy though.

F: That's a shame – maybe next time!

12 You will hear two friends talking about some changes in their sports club.

M: Have you stopped going to the sports club?

F: I haven't been for a while. It's the new changing rooms. When I go to the gym I have to use the same ones as people using the swimming pool and the floor's always wet.

M: But you could use those rooms near the squash courts – they're OK.

F: I know, but they're on the other side of the building.

M: Well, the new facilities are better for families, so that's a good thing.

F: You may be right, but until they do something about the floor, I won't go.

13 You will hear two friends talking about a new shopping centre.

M: I went to that new shopping centre yesterday – I was impressed!

F: It's certainly easy to get to, and not far away either.

M: I live on the other side of the town, so for me it was a longer drive. There's no problem parking, though – that's really good.

F: I went by bus because there's a free one from the town centre. I think it's definitely going to attract lots of people and it will probably take customers away from the town.

M: Everyone will love the range of shops – there's loads more choice than in town.

F: I'll still use the town shops, though.

LISTENING

Part 3

 PE03

Hi everyone – I want to tell you about visiting Landins Castle. It's partly a ruin so I didn't think it would be very interesting, but I was wrong.

First of all, although I knew the size of the place was impressive, because I'd seen pictures of it online, and that it had to be strong, I didn't realise that the location was so important. The castle's on top of a hill which meant that the people who lived there were safe from anyone attacking it.

It's looked after well and there's lots of information to read. There are guides who know all about the history, especially the battles. I didn't like hearing about those but I listened to one guide for ages because she was telling stories about the princesses who lived in the castle.

You can walk all round the old walls and through a formal garden then climb up into the central tower. I liked that the best because you could see so far from the top.

Because the castle's so old there aren't many complete rooms left but I was pleased that part of the main building's been restored and some of it's already been made into a café. I enjoyed the light lunch I had there! Next year they're going to open a shop.

I thought the entrance ticket might be expensive but actually family tickets are only £15 because there's a discount of £5. I went with a friend and we paid £8 each. I thought that was good value for money.

One thing I didn't know was that next summer there will be concerts there and I'm certainly planning to go to a few! I picked up some leaflets about all the entertainment and apparently there will be plays as well, though I'm not so keen on that idea.

LISTENING

Part 4

 PE04

F: Today I'm talking to Jacamo Gomes, a young dancer who has just joined a professional ballet company. Jacamo, why dance?

M: As a child I was into different kinds of sport, including football and hockey. I was especially good at gymnastics and was pretty competitive. Dancing's very satisfying, though – it gives you so much more than sport. You can create a really strong connection between the movement and the music, even if it's not always my favourite soundtrack.

F: What gave you the idea of being a dancer?

M: One day I had nothing to do so I went to a hip hop class with a friend. The teacher said I had natural talent for dancing and should do more. I wasn't keen but went again, this time to try other types of dance. As soon as I tried ballet, I realised I loved it and wanted to take it seriously and make it a career, so I applied to ballet school.

F: What should a dancer focus on when training?

M: You probably expect me to say the movements, but there are other things. Dancing is challenging physically and mentally. If you don't have a real passion for it, you won't succeed because the training is tiring and the teachers are always correcting you. This can worry you and then you can't do your best.

F: Have you entered any dance competitions?

M: Just one, when I was fourteen. My teachers helped me prepare special pieces but the standard of the other young dancers was very high. I couldn't believe I came first in both the classical and modern sections! That developed my confidence in what I could do at that time and also what I was capable of achieving in the future.

F: What are you looking forward to about joining a professional dance company?

M: Dancers do the same things every day and I'm used to that. It starts with class in the morning to warm up our bodies, then practise for any shows we're putting on. As I'm a new member I won't have any big roles to prepare, though. I can't wait to take on the responsibilities that come with a professional dance career. I'll need to learn when to rest and when to push myself so that I don't get over-tired.

F: Do you have any advice for other young dancers?

M: Every dance student has to go to auditions and that experience can be difficult. Everyone has rejections so that's quite normal. You have to explore every opportunity you get. No one is ever perfect, although you want to be, and you will find a company that suits your style.

SPEAKING

Part 1

 PE05

See page 106.

SPEAKING

Part 2

 PE06

See pages 107 and 108.

SPEAKING

Part 3

 PE07

See page 109.

SPEAKING

Part 4

 PE08

See page 110.

The **B1 Preliminary** qualification is one of the Cambridge English Qualifications. It is made up of **four** papers, each testing a different area of ability in English. The papers are Reading, Writing, Speaking and Listening, and each carries 25 percent of the marks. Candidates are awarded a score for each of the four skills and an overall score for the exam, plus a final grade (A, B or C). If a candidate's performance is below level B1, but is within level A2, the candidate will receive a Cambridge English certificate stating that they demonstrated ability at A2 level.

Reading and Use of English	45 minutes	
Writing	45 minutes	
Listening	35 minutes (approximately)	
Speaking	12–17 minutes (approximately – for each pair of students)	

All the examination questions are task-based. Rubrics (instructions) are important and should be read carefully. They set the context and give important information about the tasks. All the tasks in the exam, and all the texts you read and listen to, have been specially chosen to reflect the interests and experience of school-age learners of English.

Paper	Format	Task focus
Reading 7 Parts 52 questions	**Part 1:** Multiple choice (short texts) Choosing the correct multiple-choice answer for five short texts.	Understanding the main message.
	Part 2: Multiple matching Matching descriptions of five people with one of eight short texts.	Understanding specific information and the detailed meaning of descriptions.
	Part 3: Multiple choice (longer text) You read one longer text and answer five multiple-choice questions, each with four options to choose from.	Understanding the detailed meaning of the text, and the attitude and opinions of the writer.
	Part 4: Gapped text You read one longer text from which five sentences have been removed. Six sentences are listed after the text. You complete the text with the correct sentence in each gap.	Understanding how texts are organised and how the sentences in a text relate to each other.
	Part 5: Multiple-choice cloze You read one short text from which six words have been removed. You choose the missing word from a choice of four listed after the text.	Understanding particular words and phrases and also how words are used together to create meaning.
	Part 6: Open cloze You read one short text from which six words have been removed. You decide which word is needed to fill each gap.	Understanding how sentences are constructed and how the words and phrases in a text relate to each other.
	Part 7: Multiple matching Deciding which of the short extracts or paragraphs contains given information or ideas and matching these with ten prompts.	Reading to locate specific information, detail, opinion and attitude.
Writing 2 Parts	**Part 1:** Email You read an input text and write an email in reply to it. You have to write about 100 words and answer the points raised in the input text.	Writing an email in an appropriate style that successfully responds to points raised in the input text.
	Part 2: Article or Story Writing either an article or a story, in 100 words. There is a short input text for the article, and the first line is given for the story.	Using a range of language to create a piece of well-organised writing in a particular style.
Listening 4 tasks 25 questions	**Part 1:** Multiple choice (pictures) Answering one multiple-choice question about seven short recordings. For each recording, there is a question and three pictures. You choose the picture which bests answers the question.	Understanding specific information in announcements and simple conversations.
	Part 2: Multiple choice You listen to six short recordings and answer one multiple-choice question on each recording. You choose the best option from a choice of three.	Understanding the gist of everyday conversations, agreement and disagreement between the speakers and their individual views.
	Part 3: Sentence or note completion You listen to an announcement or presentation and complete the gaps in sentences/notes with six pieces of missing information.	Listening for and recording specific information, such as numbers and words that are spelled out.
	Part 4: Multiple choice You listen to an interview and answer six multiple-choice questions. Each question has three options to choose from.	Understanding the detailed meaning of the interview, including the attitude and opinion of the main speaker.
Speaking 4 tasks	**Part 1:** Introduction Answering simple questions posed by the examiner.	Taking part in social conversation, answering questions about yourself.
	Part 2: Individual long turn You describe a photograph.	Using appropriate descriptive language to talk about what you can see in the photograph.
	Part 3: Collaborative task A conversation with the other candidate based on a set of pictures.	Sustaining an interaction, expressing, justifying and exchanging ideas, agreeing and disagreeing, reaching a decision.
	Part 4: Discussion Further discussion on broader topics related to the Part 3 task.	Giving and justifying opinions on a range of issues and giving reasons.

Pearson Education Limited
KAO Two
KAO Park
Hockham Way
Harlow, Essex
CM17 9SR
England
and Associated Companies throughout the world.

pearsonenglish.coml

Written by Jacky Newbrook

The right of Ashley Lodge to be identified as author of the mindfulness section of this work has been asserted by him in accordance with the Copyright, Designs and Patents Act 1988

First published 2021
Second impression 2024

ISBN: 978-1-292-39137-3

Set in Avenir Next LT Pro
Print and bound by Ashford Colour Ltd

Acknowledgements

The publishers would like to thank Mark Little for his feedback on the material through its development.

Illustration acknowledgements

Richard Jones (Beehive Illustration) 109; Carl Morris (Beehive Illustration) 51, 53, 54, 55, 56, 57; Szilvia Szakall (Beehive Illustration) 82, 85; Matt Ward (Beehive Illustration) 100, 101.

Photo acknowledgements

123RF.com: believeinme33 12; **Alamy Stock Photo:** Cavan Images 80, Chad Ehlers 107, Cherie Bridges 68, Dmytro Zinkevych 81, Federico Caputo 108, Ievgen Chepil 81, John Dambik 24, MBI 77, 80, Paul Springett B 78, RossHelen editorial 83, SeventyFour Images 79, tomborro 66; **Getty Images:** adisa/iStock 87, Aisuke Asauchi/Moment 43, andresr/E+ 47, AntonioGuillem/iStock 84, AnVr/iStock 53, Avalon_Studio 34, Ben Pipe Photography/Cultura 86, Borchee/E+ 14, Bread and Butter Productions/Photodisc 90, brusinski/iStock 16, Cavan Images 67, Corinna Kern/E+ 64, Darryl Leniuk/DigitalVision 22, Dimitri Otis/DigitalVision 59, eurobanks/iStock 90, Ezra Bailey/Stone 42, fotoVoyager/ E+ 4, 36, George Clerk/E+ 14, georgeclerk/E+ 49, GMVozd/E+ 142, Hispanolistic/E+ 33, Image Source/Photodisc 96, James O'Neil/The Image Bank 39, John Burke/Stockbyte 27, John Lamb/The Image Bank 43, Kiratsinh Jadeja/Stone 90, Lane Oatey/Blue Jean Images 55, m-imagephotography/iStock 90, Maskot 4, 31, 35, Matjaz Slanic/E+ 60, Mekdet/ Moment 30, mel-nik/iStock 50, mihtiander/iStock 26, Monty Rakusen/Cultura 44, MundusImages/E+ 143, Peter Dazeley/The Image Bank 28, Prasit photo/Moment 97, Roberto Westbrook 69, shironosov/iStock 5, 37, Silvia P/EyeEm 73, sturti/E+ 25, The Good Brigade/DigitalVision 52, Thomas Barwick/Stone 15, Tim Robberts/Stone 16, Tom Werner/ DIgitalVision 90, Uwe Krejci/Photodisc 16, vgajic/E+ 13, Vladimir Vladimirov/E+ 21, vm 72, wagnerokasaki/E+ 16, Westend61 48, wundervisuals/E+ 5, 38, Yagi Studio/Photodisc 16, Yusuke Nishizawa/DigitalVision 51; **Shutterstock.com:** 75, 76, Elizaveta Galitckaia 70, EverGrump 61, fizkes 61, Iulian Valentin 61, Jacob Lund 75, Joshua Rainey Photography 9, Micha Weber 8, oliveromg 80, Sam Wordley 12, WAYHOME studio 61

Text Credit(s):

Extract on page 68 adapted from The plastics campaigner that changed the way we think about our oceans, The Telegraph, 19/11/2018, (Robbie Hodges), copyright © Telegraph Media Group Limited

All other images © Pearson Education